Coaching Questions

A Coach's Guide to Powerful Asking Skills

By Tony Stoltzfus

ISBN 978-0-9794-1636-1

Cover Design by Mark Neubauer

Some of the anecdotal illustrations in this book are true to life, and are included with the permission of the persons involved. All others are composites of real situations, and any resemblance to persons living or dead is coincidental.

For additional copies
of this book and other
coaching and coach
training materials,
visit our web site at:

www.Coach22.com

Table of Contents

Table of Contents

Introduction

"Can you give us some more examples great coaching questions? Do you have a list of the questions that you use that you could share with us?"

Fielding that request over and over provided the original impetus to write this book. I decided to respond by sharing some of the great questions I've collected and used (or that popped into my head during key moments) with you.

But upon further reflection, I realized that I could do much more than just provide lists of questions. Many coaching queries are attached to specific asking tools. For instance, if I inquire of a client, "What's your ideal role? Draw me a picture of that," I am employing the skill of visualization. By asking for an answer couched in visual language (i.e. "Draw me a picture…"), I'm helping create a description of the future the person can see, touch, get inside of, and actually experience. That's compelling!

The question works because it is built on the idea that experiential, visual pictures touch us deeply, and therefore motivate us to change. So I ask the question in *this* particular way because creating a compelling, exciting, energizing picture of the future jump-starts the change process. Once you understand the visualization technique (see pg. 42) and why a coach might use it, you'll be able to construct your own visualization questions, and you won't need a question list.

Can You Do It?

At least, that's the theory. Now that I've explained this technique, come up with five alternate ways to ask a visualization question in the next 45 seconds (and don't start with, "Draw me a picture"—I already gave you that one). Hurry up—the client is waiting for your next question!

Making use of a new skill in real coaching situations is harder than it sounds. If you've mastered an asking technique in the past, the question will come to you effortlessly in the moment, as your mind draws on stored memories from how you've done it before. However, when you try a new skill, you don't have those stored memories to draw from, and you're a lot more likely to freeze up or draw a blank.

Leveraging Short-Term Memory

In that type of situation, a list of sample questions can be extremely helpful: to load up your short-term memory to use in place of the long-term memories of an experienced coach (which you may not have yet!). And that's the best way to use this book. It's written as a series of "cheat sheets" designed to help you quickly brush up on your skills. When you need to master a new tool or make use of an unfamiliar technique, simply flip to that section of the book and *briefly* review it before you use it. A few minutes spent loading some phrases into your short-term memory will give you enough cues to spontaneously generate the right question in the moment.

For example, let's say you have a coaching session coming up this afternoon where the GROW conversational model would be a perfect fit. However, you haven't used it for months, and you're feeling less than confident that you can do it smoothly. So flip to the GROW section in this book, take a few extra minutes before your appointment to review it, and you'll feel much more up to speed.

Memory Jogging, not Memorization

The first time you try a new skill like a conversational model, you might choose to leave the book open for reference while you practice. But from then on, do a quick review and then *close the book while you coach!* The idea of the question lists is not that you memorize them, or

Application

An overview of the book and how to get the most out of it.

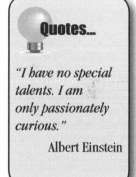

Quotes…

"I have no special talents. I am only passionately curious."

Albert Einstein

that you scan through a canned list of questions while the client is on the phone (that will make your coaching pretty stilted). What we're doing is loading up your memory with some question fragments and a sense of what might work, so in the moment the right question will come to you. In essence, we're duplicating how your long-term memory would work if you'd used this technique many times. That's why a quick review is best: you want to give your mind enough raw material that you can create your own question in the moment, without studying the examples so long that you tend to spit them back word for word.

Where to Use This Book

Coaching Questions can be a great resource for new coaches, coaches in training, or those who coach less frequently or in volunteer roles. Here's how to use it:

- ### A Training Aid For Students
  Coaching Questions is a great aid while you're in a formal coach training program. When you are working on a particular technique like "Five Options" (pg. 41), take 30 seconds to review the sample questions, close the book, and then practice it on a peer. You'll be better able to focus on what the client is saying (instead of trying to think up your next question). And the more confident and effective you are, the faster you'll learn.

- ### A Skill- and Confidence-Booster for New Coaches
  This book contains dozens of practical aids any coach can put to use immediately. To grow in a particular area, find an applicable tool, and then use the practice exercises to build your skills. Added competence quickly translates into the confidence you need to market your services and build a successful practice. We've even provided a independent study course of exercises ("Become a Master of Asking"; pg. 10) so you can continue your coaching education.

- ### A Brush-up for Part-Time Coaches
  If coaching is a part-time pursuit for you (for instance, you coach a few key employees or as a volunteer in your church), a few minutes with this book before each appointment can significantly boost your confidence and effectiveness. Instead of gradually losing the skills you gained in coach training, you'll find yourself retaining them and even adding new ones.

- ### A Toolkit for Experienced Coaches
  If you are a professional coach, you'll find new tools (and new ways to apply the ones you already know). Scan the question lists to discover fresh ways to ask familiar questions. Part of being a great coach is continuing to learn and grow in your capabilities. *Coaching Questions* lets you glean from the great asking techniques of other experienced coaches.

Wherever you are starting from, dive right in, and find the tools that will take you to the next step on your asking journey!

Becoming a Coach

As a reference tool focusing specifically on building asking skills, this book doesn't cover everything you need to learn to become a coach. For instance, it assumes you grasp the values and principles behind coaching, as well as other core skills like listening and accountability. For a comprehensive introduction to coaching (and a great companion to this book), try *Leadership Coaching*, also by Tony Stoltzfus (available through Coach22.com).

I: Getting Started

Questions have the power to change lives. They can jump-start creativity, change our perspective, empower us to believe in ourselves, push us to think things through or call us to action. This handbook of asking tools is designed to strengthen your ability to meet each moment in your coaching conversations with powerful, incisive questions.

Finding What You Need

As a reference guide, this book is designed to be flipped through and consulted for specific needs instead of being read cover to cover. It's a handbook you can return to again and again to brush up, practice a specific skill or fill a hole in your training. To find just what you need, start with the table of contents on page four. It's divided into six sections:

- **Getting Started**
  Learn about the power of asking, how to fix the top asking mistakes coaches make, and explore the tools used in forming the relational alliance with a new coachee.

- **The Coaching Process**
  Asking tools for the fundamental steps of the coaching process. This section covers conversational models, goal setting, exploration, options, and action plans.

- **Life Coaching: Destiny Discovery**
  Tools, exercises and examples for discovering and aligning with one's purpose in life. Built around a life purpose model of Design, Passion, Experience and Calling.

- **Life Coaching: A Better Life Today**
  Tools and question examples for identifying what the gaps in life are, and for making decisions to live a balanced, healthy lifestyle.

- **Advanced Tools**
  Asking skills for taking your coaching to the next level. Includes topics like challenge, reframing, motivation and more.

- **Coaching Niches**
  Short articles and examples that highlight the unique approaches used in a wide range of coaching specialties.

Instead of just listing the chapters, this table of contents breaks down each section into individual skills (usually consisting of one to three pages of tools and examples).

Index and Cross References

Most pages include a "For More" box in the bottom of the sidebar with cross-reference links that let you easily jump to a different page with more tools or examples for that particular topic. Finally, a topical index (see pg. 98) in the back of the book helps you find a particular tool or explore a topic that appears in multiple places throughout the book.

Section Overview

Section I takes an overall look at the discipline of asking, covers the kinds of questions coaches ask when setting up a coaching relationship, and includes some key questions to look at if you are developing a marketing plan or choosing a coaching school. The questions you ask when you are forming the coaching alliance set the tone for everything that's to come, so this is a great place to start on the journey of building great asking skills.

Why Ask?

Why ask questions, anyway?

What's the benefit of using coaching questions instead of advising or telling in a mentor or consultant role? Quite simply, questions hold the power to cause us to think, create answers we believe in, and motivate us to act on our ideas. Asking moves us beyond passive acceptance of what others say, or staying stuck in present circumstances, to aggressively applying our creative ability to the problem.

Questions also redefine relationships between people. When I am advising, mentoring or consulting, I'm the expert. My role makes me your superior (at least in knowledge). But when I'm asking you for your ideas, I'm a peer. Questions honor you as a person and communicate your value as an equal.

And because this asking approach changes the relationship, it also changes *you*. Have you ever left a conversation thinking, "Boy, that conversation was one-sided! The whole thing was about him." My wife calls that a lack of "conversational generosity". We all hate it when others can't stop talking about their own thoughts and ideas—but we're blind to how often we do it ourselves.

The coaching approach forces your conversations to become less about your thoughts, your input, and how you can steer the dialogue around to the answer you think will work. You start listening—*really listening*—to the other person. You decrease what you say, so that others can increase. And that's where the magic happens: the more you listen, the more you see how capable they are, how much they can do with a little encouragement, and what wonderful individuals they are. The more you ask, the more you love.

Look Smart

"On a trip to another country, I visited a college with Dave, a friend of the president of that institution. He was out, so Dave sat me down in the president's office and went to do some other business. Meanwhile, the president showed up unexpectedly. I introduced myself and after an awkward moment, I began asking him questions about the students at the college: 'What part of the country did they come from? What do they study? What do they do after they graduate?'

It turns out that one-third of the students are sent out by the college do to community service. That piqued my curiosity, so I asked, 'Where do they go? What do they do in the villages? Are they achieving their mission? How is it funded? How is that sustainable?' For 20 minutes the president talked while I asked questions.

Suddenly, Dave popped his head into the office, greeted the president and said to me, 'Keith, we've got to go—our class is beginning'; so I said my good-byes. Later, Dave mentioned that the president was very impressed with me. 'I learned so much from Keith about community service projects,' he said. 'Please ask him to come and teach a course here.'

Dave was amazed when I explained that I had only asked questions."

Keith Webb, Creative Results Management

Five Great Reasons to Ask

We've been talking about the heart behind the asking approach. There are practical reasons to adopt coaching questions as well. Here are five key reasons to ask instead of tell:

1. All the Information is with the Coachee

Nobody knows more about you than you. Since all the memories of your life are stored in your head, you are the resident expert on you. So if you are, say, trying to improve your relationship with a co-worker, you can call up years of memories of working with that person, list what you've tried so far or what's worked with others in the past, describe the organizational culture at your workplace, etc. The coach has none of that information. The coachee always knows far more about the situation than the coach.

2. Asking Creates Buy-In

Coaching starts with the assumption that the key to change is not knowing what to do—its being motivated to do it. Research shows (and experience confirms) that people are more motivated to carry out their own ideas and solutions. What that means is that a less-optimal solution the coachee develops often produces better results than the "right" answer coming from the coach. Asking creates buy-in, and buy-in gets results.

3. Asking Empowers

I've made an interesting discovery as a coach. People often ask for coaching to help them make a major decision. But roughly 80% of the time, I find that they already know what to do: they just don't have the confidence to step out and do it. Self-confidence is a huge factor in change. When you ask for people's opinions and take them seriously, you are sending a powerful message: "You have great ideas. I believe in you. You can do this." Just asking can empower people to do things they couldn't do on their own.

4. Asking Develops Leadership Capacity

Leadership is the ability to take responsibility. A leader is someone who sees a problem, and says, "Hey—someone needs to do something about this! And I'm going to be that someone." Simply asking, "What could *you* do about that?" moves people away from depending on you for answers, and toward taking leadership in the situation. Asking builds the responsibility muscle, and that develops leaders.

5. Asking Creates Authenticity

We all want to be known, and loved. There is no greater relational gift than to have someone see the real you and value it. The art of asking creates a bond between us and those we coach, because by asking we honor and value them. Taking the time to ask significant questions (and listen to the answers!) communicates that we really want to know who they are at a deep level. This asking approach is the quickest way to build trust and transparency between people. And when we talk about the things our clients really care about, they make changes that are truly transformational.

For More

Become a "Master of Asking"

Think of the "Master of Asking" schedule as a ten-week weight-lifting program for your asking muscles. It's a self-study course you can work through with a peer coach to increase your proficiency in asking coaching questions. Each week includes a 60 to 75 minute phone or in-person peer session where you practice on each other, along with one exercise to try out on your own during the week with a friend, family member or a client.

Exercises	Time
Week 1: Open Questions　　　　Date: _____	
☐ Set dates and times for the rest of your sessions and record in your datebooks.	5 min
☐ Do the *Conversation Starters* exercise on page 19.	20 min
☐ Do the *Broad Questions* exercise (pg. 38) together. Then take turns posing narrow questions and asking your partner to make them broader.	20 min
☐ Do the *Observation and Question* exercise on page 40. Debrief afterward using the debriefing procedure in the sidebar (at left).	30 min
☐ On Your Own: Find three opportunities this week to use a conversation starter. Prepare to do a practice comp session next week with your peer partner.	
Week 2: Comp Sessions　　　　Date: _____	
☐ Take turns doing the *Comp Session* exercise on page 21 with your partner, then debrief. What do you need to improve to be more effective?	75 min
☐ On Your Own: Use the *Marketing Plan* exercise on page 17 to sharpen your comp session presentation.	
Week 3: Life Wheel and SMART Goals　　　　Date: _____	
☐ Take turns doing the *Life Wheel* exercise (pg. 34) with your partner. Debrief.	35 min
☐ Coach each other through creating a one-sentence SMART goal statement (pg. 37) from the agenda you chose with the *Life Wheel*. Debrief.	25 min
☐ On Your Own: Do the *Life Wheel* with a friend, client or family member.	
Week 4: Options　　　　Date: _____	
☐ Identify a practical challenge or change issue in your own life, then take turns coaching each other using the *Five Options Technique* (pg. 41). Debrief.	30 min
☐ Identify a dream you'd like to pursue; then coach each other through the *Ideal Future Technique* (pg. 42). Create a *rich, visual* picture of the ideal. Debrief.	45 min
☐ On Your Own: Ask your spouse or a good friend to share a dream s/he would like to pursue, then coach the person through the *Ideal Future Technique*.	
Week 5: Options Part II　　　　Date: _____	
☐ Identify a place in life where you are stuck or struggling. Coach each other using the *Obstacle Approach* (pg. 41). Debrief.	35 min
☐ Try the *Transformational Approach* or *Thinking Outside the Box* (pg. 42-43) on the same issue. What new ideas do you come up with? Debrief.	35 min
☐ On Your Own: Try one of these approaches with a client this week.	

Week 6: Conversational Models Date: _____	
☐ Take 25 to 30 minutes each to coach each other through the *GROW* model using a practical life issue (pg. 28), then debrief.	75 min
☐ Evaluate your action steps using the *Four Tests* (pg. 45). How well do they fit?	
☐ On Your Own: Practice using *GROW* with at least one person this week.	
Week 7: Conversational Models II Date: _____	
☐ Take 25 to 30 minutes to coach each other through the *Coaching Funnel* (pg. 30), then debrief. What kind of issues would be best suited to each model?	75 min
☐ On Your Own: Practice using the *Coaching Funnel* at least once this week.	
Week 8: Obstacles Date: _____	
☐ Take a coaching issue where you are struggling to follow through from a previous week, and do the *Identifying Obstacles* exercise (pg. 46). Then use the *Tackling Obstacles* exercise to figure out how to overcome it. If you have extra time, repeat with another issue.	75 min
☐ On Your Own: Take the same obstacle and run yourself through several of the strategies on pages 47 and 48 that you didn't try in your peer session.	
Week 9: Top Asking Mistakes Date: _____	
☐ Take 25 minutes each to coach each other through the GROW model using a practical life issue (pg. 28). When you are finished, have your partner give feedback on how you did on each of the *Top Ten Asking Mistakes* (pg. 16).	75 min
☐ On Your Own: Pick one of the *Asking Mistakes* that you need to work on and find a place to practice implementing the solution given in the exercise.	
Week 10: Decisions and Affirmation Date: _____	
☐ Identify a significant decision you need to make. Then coach each other using the *Decision Making Strategies* exercise on page 70.	50 min
☐ Use the *Powerful Affirmation* exercise (pg. 69) to affirm what you've seen in each other as you've worked together.	25 min

Become a Master of Life Coaching

If you'd like to build a stronger repertoire of life coaching skills, sign on for another ten weeks with your peer coach and do the exercises below. You can work on the exercises on your own and then just discuss the results, but you'll get more practice if you coach your peer through the exercises right in your sessions.

Week 1: Life Purpose Inventory (pg. 51)
Week 2: Dream Inventory/ Fun List (pg. 53)
Week 3: Ideal Life (pg. 55)
Week 4: Creating and Refining Value Statements (pg. 56)
Week 5: Destiny Experiences (pg. 59)

Week 6: Whom Will I Serve and Finding Purpose in Suffering (pg. 61)
Week 7: Take It or Leave It (pg. 63)
Week 8: Energy Drains and Toleration (pg. 64-65)
Week 9: Difficult Conversations (pg. 67)
Week 10: Significant Experiences (pg. 81)

Hints & Tips

Working with a Peer Coach
One of the best ways to hone your coaching skills is to coach another coach. It keeps you on your toes when the other person knows how you are *supposed* to be doing it! If you are going through a coach training program, it's usually easy to find someone else in your cohort to work with. If you are on your own, try a coaching network or special interest group, or find a friend who wants to learn more about coaching and teach the person some of the basics as you go.

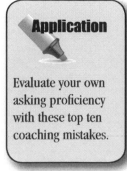

Application

Evaluate your own asking proficiency with these top ten coaching mistakes.

The Top Ten Asking Mistakes

(And How to Correct Them)

Here's a coach trainer's personal list of the top ten asking mistakes coaches make.

1. Closed Questions

Our number one offender is—closed questions! Open questions have two key benefits: they let the coachee direct the conversation (because they can be answered in many ways) and they make the coachee think by eliciting longer answers. While most people will answer the occasional closed question as if it were open, too many closed questions in a row shuts people down.

Solution: Convert Closed to Open Questions

To convert closed questions to open ones, first become aware of what you are asking. If you catch yourself before you've finished asking, stop and restate the question. You'll know a closed question because it can be answered with a simple "yes" or "no," like these examples:

- *"Is there a way to do that and still keep evenings for family?"*
- *"Can you realistically take that on too?"*
- *"Could there be any other ways to approach that?"*
- *"Do you have any other options?"*

When you catch yourself in the act of asking a closed question, here's a quick technique for adjusting: restate the question, but this time beginning with the word "what" or "how". Here are the closed questions listed above, but now made open using this technique:

- *"What could you do to still keep evenings for family?"*
- *"How would your life change if you take that on, too?"*
- *"How else could you approach that?"*
- *"What other options do you have?"*

2. Solution-Oriented Questions (SOQs)

A special kind of closed question is the solution-oriented question. SOQs are pieces of advice with a question mark pasted on. We want to tell the client the answer, but we remember we are supposed to be coaching, so we give our solution in the form of a question:

- *"Shouldn't you check in with your boss before you act on this?"*
- *"Could you do your jogging with your spouse?"*
- *"Do you think that affirming the person would give you a better result?"*
- *"Can you give her the benefit of the doubt on this one?"*

"Should you, could you, will you, don't you, can you, are you"—if the second word in the question is "you," you're in trouble.

Solution: Follow Your Curiosity

On a practical level, SOQs usually originate in an intuitive insight: something the person says makes us curious, so (all in our own heads) we proceed to identify what we think the underlying problem is, create a solution, and then offer it to the person. The trick is to go back to the thing that made you curious in the first place, and ask about that. Often this involves broadening our SOQ (which focused on one potential solution) into an open question with many possible solutions. For instance:

- Our insight on the first question listed above was wondering what the channels of authority in this organization are. So we might ask, *"In your company, what kind of channels do you need to go through before you act on this?"* (Notice how this question allows for other answers than just talking to the boss.)
- On the second question, our intuition noticed that the client is an extrovert, yet all the potential exercise options were done alone. So you might say, *"I noticed that all your exercise options were solitary activities. How could you involve other people in your exercise routine?"*

3. Seeking the "One True Question"

One of the biggest stumbling blocks for beginning coaches is the quest for the Holy Grail: the question that will unlock the secrets of the universe for the client. Before each question there is a long, awkward pause while we search our mind for just the right thing to say—and meanwhile the momentum of the conversation is lost.

Solution: Trust the Process

It's not the perfect question that makes the difference: you just need to help the person you are coaching think a little farther down the road than they will on their own. *Trust the process* to help the person, not the greatness of your insight. One excellent technique when you are starting out as a coach is to lean on a very simple query, like, *"Tell me more,"* or *"What else?"* The benefit of these short-and-sweet questions is that they don't interrupt the person's thought process at all. Another great tool is the *Observation and Question* technique. Pick out the most significant thing the person said, repeat their exact words, and ask them to expand on it, like this:

- *"You mentioned that _____. Tell me more about that."*

By varying the question (instead of *"Tell me more…,"* try *"Say more,"* or *"Expand on that,"* or *"What's going on there?"*) you can use this technique over and over without sounding stilted. It's a great way to keep the focus on the client and not on your greatness as a coach.

4. Rambling Questions

A variant of the "One True Question" problem is the rambling question. Some coaches can't stop themselves from asking the same question in three different ways, while stringing together five different nuances or potential answers along the way. By the time the coach has finally articulated the question, the client is confused about what to answer and any conversational flow is lost.

Solution: Think, then Talk

The propensity to ramble can usually be overcome in one of two ways. First, some coaches do this because they are still figuring out what they want to ask while they are asking. The solution is simple: allow it to be silent for a moment or two while you formulate the question. Our uncomfortableness with silence is leading us to jump in before we are ready

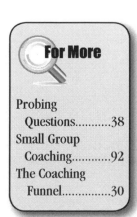

to ask. When you start doing this, you'll often find that a little silence will lead the client to continue to process without you asking any question at all.

The second common cause of rambling is that we are overly concerned that our question be fully grasped. Our need to be understood comes from trying to lead the person down a particular path (in other words, we are in telling mode). Let go of your agenda, ask the question once, stop, and see where the person chooses to take it. Often the most exciting coaching moments come when the client *doesn't* understand what you are asking for!

5. Interpretive Questions

Sometimes just by asking a question we put a spin on what the client is saying. For instance, a client says, "I'm finding it tough lately to want to get up on Monday mornings. I'm frustrated with my current project, I'm not getting the support I need, and I keep finding myself looking at the clock and wishing the day was over." A response like, *"How long have you hated your job?"* is likely to get a reaction from the client ("Wait a minute—I never said I hated my job…!") The reason? Our coaching question reveals our *interpretation* of what the client said. We don't know yet whether this person hates his job, dislikes it, or even loves it. We only know what the client said. Interpretive questions erode trust (because they put something on the client) and block the conversational flow as the person responds to our analysis.

Solution: Use Their Own Words

Interpretative questions are easy to correct: simply make a habit of incorporating the client's own words in your questions. For the example above, we might ask, *"How long have you been <u>frustrated with your current project</u>?"* or *"What kind of <u>support do you need</u> that you aren't getting?"* or *"What triggers you <u>looking at the clock and wishing the day was over</u>?"* The underlined words in these questions are taken directly from the client's own statements. Asking in this way prevents the client from reacting to your spin and keeps the conversation moving in a productive direction.

6. Rhetorical Questions

Although posed in question form, rhetorical questions are actually statements (often emotional or judgmental) of your own opinion of the situation:

- *"What were you thinking!?!"*
- *"Are you really going to throw away your career like that?"*
- *"Isn't that just a cop-out?"*
- *"Wouldn't you rather get along with your spouse?"*

Since we aren't really asking for the other person's opinion, these questions evoke either no response or a defensive one. Rhetorical questions are generally a sign that you've made a judgement or developed an attitude about the person you are coaching.

Solution: Reset Your Attitude

Eliminating rhetorical questions requires a change in attitude toward the client. One way is to get in touch with what is going on inside you, and how this situation is pushing your emotional buttons. A second approach is to renew your internal picture of the coachee's potential and ability. Spend 15 to 20 minutes on these reflection questions to reorient yourself around believing in the client:

- *"Why am I forming judgments here? How is focusing on the negative in this person meeting my own needs? What can I do about that?"*
- *"Could I be wrong about the situation? What am I missing?"* See if you can construct two possible scenarios where the coachee's point of view is more valid than your own.
- *"What potential, ability and wisdom do I see in this person? What can s/he become? Why am I drawn to coach him/her?"*

7. Leading Questions

Leading questions are ones that subtly point the coachee to a certain answer: the one the coach (knowingly or unknowingly) wants. While rhetorical questions are blatantly biased, with leading questions you may not even realize you are propelling the conversation in a certain direction. What response do you think the coach wants in the following examples?

- *"How would you describe that feeling: discouraged?"*
- *"We've spent a fair amount of time processing this over the last several weeks: are you ready to make a decision on that now?"*
- *"Do you want to stay with this organization you've invested so much in?"*
- *"It seems like this option would feel good today, but the other would give lasting satisfaction. Which one do you want to choose?"*

Solution: Multiple Options, Or the Opposite

When you catch yourself in the act of asking a leading question, you can often redeem it by creating multiple solutions. Take the leading question (like, *"Name that emotion: are you disappointed?"*), and then add several more options on the end: *"…are you disappointed, excited, upset, or what?"* With multiple options, the coachee has to choose how to respond, instead of taking the easy way out and just agreeing with you.

Another excellent technique is one I call "Or the Opposite". If you realize you've just asked a leading question (i.e. *"If you take this new position, will it take time and energy away from your family?"*), paste on an "or," and then ask the opposite question: *"…Or will this open up doors to get you the kind of family time you truly want?"*

Part of what makes these two techniques so useful is that you only have to change the very end of the question. You can realize you are asking a leading question midway through, and still change it on the fly without the client ever knowing what happened.

8. Neglecting to Interrupt

No, that's not a misprint. Being too timid to interrupt and refocus the conversation is more of a problem for beginning coaches than interrupting too much. While some clients speak concisely, others can go on for ten minutes every time you ask an open question. Too much irrelevant detail slows progress and blurs your focus.

Solution: Restore the Focus

Part of your job as a coach is managing the conversation, so when you see the client bunny-trailing, interject with a question that brings things back to focus. A pro-active step is to openly discuss the rambling issue and secure permission to interrupt when needed.

Quotes…

"The art and science of asking questions is the source of all knowledge."

Thomas Berger

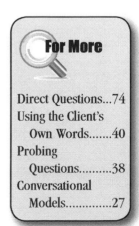

For More

- *"It caught my attention when you mentioned earlier that _____. Let's come back to that."*
- *"You are pretty good at expressing yourself. Would you mind if I interrupt occasionally to keep us on track so that we can make the most of our time?"*

9. Interrupting

The other side of the interruption coin is that for some of us (often the most verbal or relational personalities) interrupting is a habit we aren't very aware of. Frequent interrupters tend to be perceived as dishonoring and frustrating to talk to—not the kind of image you want to cultivate as a coach! Are you an interrupter? If you want to find out, here's a revealing exercise. First, record one of your coaching conversations. Then fast-forward to the middle (by then you'll have forgotten you're recording yourself), listen to the tape, and make a note every time you hear each of the three following things:

- Interruption: I interrupted or made a comment while the client was still talking
- Talking Over: I kept talking when the client tried to interrupt me; or when we both started simultaneously, I failed to defer to the client
- Talking For: I finished the client's thought for him/her

The Solution: Count to Two

Here's a simple discipline you can practice to break an interrupting habit. Make a commitment that when you are coaching you will count off two seconds ("one, one thousand; two, one thousand") after the coachee has stopped speaking before you reply or ask a question. And if the person begins speaking again before the two seconds is up, good! Your goal as a coach is not to interject your ideas, but to help the coachees explore and implement their own.

10. "Why" Questions

"Why" questions tend to make people clam up because they challenge motives. When you pose a question like, *"Why did you do that?"* you are asking the coachee to defend and justify his or her actions—so don't be surprised if s/he gets defensive!

Solution: Use "What" Instead

It's easy to rephrase questions to replace the "why" with "what". Here are several examples of "why" questions that have been reworded with "what" to keep from putting people on the defensive:

- *"Why did you turn down the job?"*
- **Better:** *"What factors led you to turn down the job?"*

- *"Why do you think she'd respond like that?"*
- **Better:** *"What's causing you to anticipate that response?"*

- *"Why can't you talk to him about that?"*
- **Better:** *"What do you need to talk to him about that?"*

Exercise: Top Ten Asking Exercises
Record a session where you are coaching, and listen for the ten common asking mistakes. It's hard to listen for all ten—you may want to focus on only three for ten minutes or so, then spend the next ten minutes listening for the next three. To keep track, list the ten mistakes on a sheet of paper, and put a tick mark next to a particular mistake each time you hear yourself make it. When you're done, pick an area to focus on and practice using the corrective strategy mentioned in the text.

Coaching Questions: A Coach's Guide to Powerful Asking Skills

A Marketing Plan in Five Questions

Answer these five sets of questions to begin designing your coaching practice, identifying your niche and creating a marketing program. It's also a great exercise to use when you're mentor-coaching another coach or working with an independent professional or businessperson. These five questions start with your best assets and connect them to felt needs of potential customers.

Application

Designing your practice or helping another person design theirs.

1. THE PRODUCTS: <u>What</u> do you have to offer?

- *"What do you excel at? What are your best skills?"*
- *"What is your niche? Where do you want to focus?"*
- *"What do you do that people are eager to pay for?"*

    Action Step: Create a list of the specific products you'll offer, including features and pricing for each one. Try to create a range of price points people can start at, and chart the ways you could up-sell your customers to other related services.

2. THE TARGET AUDIENCE: <u>Who</u> will you serve?

- *"Who is already attracted to me and sees me as a resource?"*
- *"Who am I drawn to and want to coach?"*
- *"Who needs the services I have to offer?"*

    Action Step: Create a profile of your ideal client: age, needs, life stage, gender, profession, and whatever else is relevant. Then list five places where your target audience congregates where you could connect with them.

3. KEY DISTINCTIVES: <u>Why</u> would they want your services? What do they need?

- *"What are their felt needs?"*
- *"What distinguishes you or makes you credible in their eyes in that area?"*
- *"How does what you do meet those needs? How will your service benefit them?"*

    Action Step: Make a list of the top five reasons your target audience would buy from you. Then find a way to test your thinking with some representative individuals to make sure it is valid.

4. THE PITCH: <u>How</u> will you get your message across?

- *"How will people find out about you?"*
- *"How will they learn enough about you to want to hire/buy from you?"*
- *"How will you follow up? What will you say to prospects to turn them into customers?"*

    Action Step: Create a basic strategy for getting your message to your target audience (i.e. advertising, networking, referrals, speaking, etc). Write out your plan.

5. THE PLAN: <u>When</u> will you start?

- *"What is my plan of action?"*
- *"What do I need to do first?"*
- *"When will I start designing my practice? By when will I have launched it?"*

    Action Step: Develop an action plan that lays out step-by-step how you'll use this strategy to launch your practice. Put target dates by the phases of your launch process.

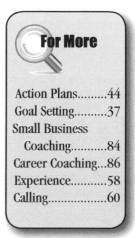

A coaching question can be a great way to take everyday conversations from surface to significance. Instead of asking, *"How are you?"* or *"What's new with you these days?"* and getting the standard replies, take a risk and ask about something you really care about.

Icebreakers

These icebreakers are good for launching a conversation with someone you've just met. A great strategy is to take a common question that people are comfortable with, then ask a follow-up question that makes the conversation a little more intimate.

- *"How are you today?"* When they answer "Fine" or "Good," come back with, *"What makes today a fine day?"*
- *"What do you do for a living?"* Then, *"What do you like best about your job?"*
- *"What's something memorable about you, that I can remember you by?"*
- *"Tell me a little about your family."* Then, *"What's something you love to do with them?"*
- *"Where are you from?"* Then, *"What's been your favorite place to live? Why?"*
- *"What brings you here today? What do you hope to gain from this* [trip, event, situation, etc]*?"*
- *"How's your day going?"* Then, *"What's been the high point so far?"*

Significant Questions

Significant questions go a little deeper than icebreakers: they make people think about something important, draw out a person's identity or touch their deepest desires. These questions are an excellent way to launch a coaching conversation, or you can use them with friends, family members, at parties or at networking events. Learn to ask significant questions and you can have memorable, life-changing conversations with just about anyone! Below are several types of significant questions, with examples for each.

Significance

- *"What's the most significant thing that's happened in your life in the last month?"*
- *"What's the best thing about your life right now? (And what's one thing you'd love to change?)"*
- *"What is on your mind this week? What are you thinking about?"*
- *"What's the growing edge for you as a leader these days?"*
- *"Name one great joy and one sorrow that you've experienced this year."*

Identity

- *"Tell me a story from your life that would give me a picture of who you really are. What is an event that shaped you as a person?"*
- *"What's been the most interesting spiritual encounter you've had in your life?"*
- *"Tell me about someone who has helped you become the person you are today. Who has really influenced your life, and how?"*
- *"If you could go back in time and meet any historical figure, who would it be, and why?"*
- *"Name two or three of your best strengths. What are you really great at?"*

Deepest Desires

- *"What's your dream? If you could do anything with your life, what would you do?"*
- *"What do you want these days? What are you passionately pursuing or longing for?"*
- *"If one burden could be removed from you today, what would that be?"*
- *"If you had unlimited resources, what would you most want to do with them?"*
- *"What's your greatest joy right now? Your greatest fear? Your greatest challenge?"*

Conversation Starters for Organizational Leaders

- *"What was the best thing that happened this month in your sphere of influence? What one thing would you like to change?"*
- *"What dreams do you have for the future of your organization?"*
- *"What's the best thing about working with this* [company, team, project]*?"*
- *"What's the greatest asset of your organization or team? Your biggest challenge?"*
- *"What's one thing you need to move your team to the next level that you don't currently have?"*
- *"If you could wave a magic wand and change any one thing about your company, what would that be? What led you to choose that?"*
- *"What is bringing you 80% of your joy as a leader? What is bringing you 80% of your stress?"*
- *"Why do you care about this organization? What makes your job significant?"*
- *"How does this job bring out the best in you?"*

Hints & Tips

A great question can put someone on the defensive if they aren't anticipating being coached. You may want to ask permission before you try out your coaching techniques on an unsuspecting family member!

Exercise: Conversation Starters

Here's a great way to practice starting significant conversations in a group (it's also a wonderful party game). Give everyone a copy of five or six of these questions. Then have the group stand up and pair off. Each person asks their partner a significant question, then after three minutes, you switch places and have the second person ask the question. Set a kitchen timer or your watch to buzz every three minutes. Once both partners have gotten a chance to ask a question, switch partners and do another round with a different person. You can do as many rounds as you like.

Effective Comp Sessions

Most professional coaches offer a short complimentary coaching session to potential clients. It's a way to let people kick the tires, ask questions, and talk about what they want. And it's a chance for you to present coaching to an interested individual. There are several things you want to accomplish in a comp session:

1. **Connection.** Make a personal connection. Find the spark of chemistry with each other.
2. **Motivation.** The heart of the comp session. Explore what the client is highly motivated to pursue, and how you can help .
3. **Presentation.** Take their specific need, and show how coaching can help meet it.
4. **Information.** Provide any information the prospective client needs to make a decision
5. **Decision.** Ask for a commitment.

1. Connection

A key element in a coaching relationship is chemistry. Getting to know the details of each other's lives unearths the points of connection that create a bond. Genuine curiosity, intent listening, and an excitement about the opportunity to work together create a spark that makes people want to work with you.

- *"Tell me a little about yourself."*
- *"Give me a quick sketch of who you are, and I'll do the same for you."*
- *"What led you to want to pursue a coaching relationship?"*

2. Motivation

An important objective of the comp session is to discuss the coachee's change agenda. An important dream to reach for (or a major frustration you've tolerated for too long) provides a compelling reason to be coached. Once you've tapped into a passion, help the person understand how working with a coach can help make the future they want a reality.

- *"What are the top three challenges you face right now? The top opportunities?"*
- *"What is the biggest change you'd like to make in your life right now? What would it be worth to you to make that change?"*
- *"What do you need to reach that objective that you don't have?"*
- *"What's motivating you right now—either dissatisfaction with what is or a desire to pursue something in your future?"*
- *"What 's your hesitation about starting a coaching relationship?"*
- *"What are you passionate about pursuing, and what are you eager to leave behind?"*
- *"What outcome would make this coaching relationship a great success in your eyes?"*

3. Presentation

Once you've asked the client what they are looking for, talk a little about expectations. Ask what they want in a coach, explain what you are most passionate about, and explore the fit.

- *"What would a great coach for you look like?"*
- *"Here's an example of how I helped someone like you…"*
- *"Here's how I work with that kind of goal…"*

- *"Here's what I do best as a coach…"*
- *"Does what I just described about my passion as a coach sound like what you are looking for?"*
- *"Here's what you can expect if you work with me…"*

4. Information

If you've done the first three steps well, often the person is nearly sold already. Now briefly fill in the details they need to make a decision. If the person is new to coaching, you may need to take time to describe or even briefly demonstrate it. Here are some points to cover:

- How often we will meet, and for how long
- What we'll do in a typical session
- Call procedure
- What is expected of you in between sessions
- How you'll relate with each other
- Fees and payment procedure

5. Decision

Salespeople are trained to ask in such a way as to get a "Yes" (in other words, to ask leading questions!) As coaches, while we want people to sign up, it is vital that our clients have full buy-in for the decision to be coached, so we can work with them out of their internal motivation. Don't be afraid to ask for a commitment, but do it in a way that maximizes buy-in:

- *"Is there anything else that you need to know to make a decision about a coaching relationship?"*
- *"How do you want to proceed?"*
- *"Are you ready to say, 'Yes!' to a coaching relationship, or would you like to explore further?"*
- *"What is holding you back from making a decision?"*
- *"What step would you like to take out of this conversation to keep moving forward?"*

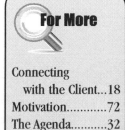

Hints & Tips

Make sure and provide some value up front during the comp session. You might share an intuitive insight, a tool, or coach the person briefly on one aspect of his/her change agenda. Providing value increases your credibility and their confidence that working with you could be a life-changing experience.

Comp Session Exercise

Do a practice comp session with a friend, peer or spouse. Afterwards, ask for feedback:

- Have the person repeat back to you what you said you have to offer as a coach. Did they get it?
- Did this person feel coaching could meet his or her felt needs after hearing your presentation? Why or why not?
- What did (or didn't) you do to create a safe, engaging, attractive atmosphere in the complimentary session?
- Discuss how you approached asking the person to sign up (you did ask, right?). How could you improve the way you ask for a commitment?

For More

Application

Questions you can use to create a Client Profile Form (or just to get to know someone's heart.)

Client Profile Form

Many coaches ask new clients to provide a personal profile before their first appointment. Profile questions can cover the client's change agenda, needs, values, desired future, assessment results, and more. What you ask depends on your coaching niche (life, business, relationship, etc.) and how you conduct your comp sessions. Here are some examples of profile questions:

Life Purpose

- *"Sketch out what you know of your own life purpose. What were you made to do?"*
- *"How well do your current roles fit or not fit with your purpose and natural strengths?"*
- *"What are some important dreams that you would like to pursue in the next five or ten years?*

Values and Priorities

- *"What is most important to you in life (or in your business)?"*
- *"Take the eight basic life areas (career, family/relationships, health, money, spirituality, personal development, recreation, and physical environment), and jot down what you care about most in each area."*
- *"In these eight areas, what are some fundamental values you base important decisions on?"*
- *"What's priority for you right now?"*
- *"In the short term, what objectives or areas of life do you most want to work on or pay attention to?*

Self-Knowledge

- *"If you've taken a personality type assessment (i.e. DiSC, Myers-Briggs, Strengths-Finder, etc.), what were the results? What did it tell you about yourself?"*
- *"List at least five important strengths you use often, and three weaknesses."*
- *"What's best about you? List five things you love about yourself."*
- *"What major changes have taken place in your life in the past six months?"*

Needs

- *"Right now I feel the greatest sense of need for…"*
- *"The problems or challenges I most want to overcome right now are..."*
- *"The things that sap my energy that I most want to remove from my life are..."*
- *"The place I feel stuck is..."*

Coaching Agenda

- *"I want to explore these possibilities in our first session or two: _____."*
- *"I want to build on these strengths or increase these skills: _____."*
- *"The tangible outcome I want from being coached is: _____."*
- *"I want to be challenged to grow in this area: _____."*
- *"I want to look at changing my thinking patterns or beliefs around: _____."*
- *"What I most desire from my coach is: _____."*

Hints & Tips

To quickly create your own customized Client Profile Form, just pick a set of questions from this page and add the standard contact info questions, put them on your letterhead and you're there!

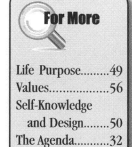

For More

Life Purpose.........49
Values.................56
Self-Knowledge
   and Design........50
The Agenda..........32
Life Wheel............33

Coaching Session Structure

Opening Chat/Care Questions

Coach trainees often ask, "What exactly goes on in a coaching session?" A good practice is to begin the conversation with a significant, open question that leaves room for the client to voice whatever is on their mind. For instance, in one past session a client was ready to dive right into his work-related change goal—until an open question brought to light that his fiancee had broken off their engagement the night before.

- *"What's been the highlight (or low-light) of your week?"*
- *"What's the most interesting thing that is going on with you right now?"*
- *"What's the most significant thing that's happened with you since we last met?"*
- *"What's new that you'd like to share?"*

Progress Report

The progress report is a brief, three to five minute overview of the action steps from the last session. Doing a quick overview of the client's work at the start is a great way to make sure you don't start talking about one item and run out of time for the others. Even though you'll have these steps written down, you'll want to work from the coachee's action list.

- *"Give me a brief progress report on your action steps."*
- *"Bring me up to speed on what you've accomplished since we last met on your action items."*

Set Agenda

Take any actions from your prior session which may require follow-up steps and discuss them. Note any new or continuing action steps. Then revisit the overall coaching goals and focus on what needs to be done to keep moving forward.

- *"Which action steps from last time do we need to create follow-up steps for?"*
- *"Are there any of these steps we need to discuss further?"*
- *"What do we need to focus on today to keep you moving toward your goals?"*
- *"What is on your agenda today? What do we need to make sure we talk about?"*

From this point on, use a conversational model such as GROW (pg. 28) to work through the coaching agenda and develop a new set of action items.

Review Action Items

Go back over the action steps you've agreed on in the session so you are both clear about what you're going to do.

- *"Give me a run down of the action steps you've listed just to make sure we both have them."*
- *"So—what are your action steps for this next week?"*

Application

An outline of the basic steps that would be covered in a normal coaching appointment.

Hints & Tips

Some coaches create a list of action items after each appointment and e-mail it to the client. Others ask the client to create the list and send it to the coach. Either practice ensures that the client is taking notes, and that you both know what steps are to be taken.

For More

Application

A procedure and set of example questions for designing your own Session Prep Form.

Session Prep Form

An easy way to add value to your coaching sessions is to use a session prep form. It's a simple set of questions the client journals on before a session to summarize what's happened since the last coaching appointment. Here are several benefits of using a prep form:

- You don't have to take time in your session for a progress report
- You have time to digest what is happening in the client's life before you meet
- It provides additional structure for the client to remember and report on steps
- The client does some structured reflection about the session beforehand and comes prepared

To create a personalized session prep form, just pick a question from each category.

Accomplishments/Celebration

- *"What have I accomplished since our last session?"*
- *"What are my wins or victories since we last met?"*
- *"What am I thankful for this week?"*

Challenges

- *"What challenges am I facing right now?"*
- *"What's going on in my life right now that I want to talk to my coach about?"*
- *"What obstacles have I run into since we last met that I want to troubleshoot?"*

Accountability

- *"Briefly list your progress on each of your action steps."*
- *"What did I not get done, but want to be held accountable for?"*
- *"What tasks have I completed or made progress on? Where did I get stuck?"*

Outcomes

- *"What do I need to focus on today to keep moving toward my goals?"*
- *"How do I want to use my coach today?"*
- *"What do I want to get out of this session?"*

Hints & Tips

Make sure and request that the Session Prep Form is returned to you at least 24 hours before an appointment so you have time to review it.

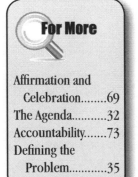

For More

Client Profile and Prep Form Exercise

If you aren't using a Client Profile (see pg. 22) and Session Prep Form, maybe it's time to give it a try. First, take half an hour or so and create your forms using the questions here and on page 22. Once you have the forms, the easiest way to start using them is to begin with a new client. Next time you pick up a client, assign the Client Profile as an action step before your first appointment. From there, it's an easy step to replace it with the Prep Form before your second appointment and make that a part of your normal procedure.

Note: Some questions contributed by Jerome Daley, www.PurposeCoach.net

Choosing a Coach Training School

Here's a question I am asked all the time: "Which coach training program should I go through?" Since (as a coach) I like to make people think instead of just giving advice, here are four questions I use to help prospective coaches decide, with a bonus hint in the sidebar:

1. Who do you want to coach?

The most important question in choosing a training program is knowing who your target audience is. It does make a difference: some schools focus on training coaches to work with business leaders, others focus on therapists who want to add coaching to their practices, while still others focus on career coaching, ministry coaching or other specialties. A school in your target area will train you using the tools and lingo you'll actually coach with. Completing a school in another specialty may give you a great education in the basics, but could also leave you wanting in the area of tools and applications.

2. What learning style suits you best?

There are a variety of training methods used by the different coaching schools, and each has advantages and disadvantages. Academic programs give you a two-fer with an advanced degree, but you may need to jump through hoops (lots of reading, writing papers, etc.) that are not really building your core skills. Skills develop quickest in workshops, because they allow for live practice with feedback. But unless they are hosted where you live, travel time and costs can be a barrier. You can join a tele-class from anywhere, so these programs are tops in convenience. However, dozens of people on one phone line is not an optimal learning environment (look for a cohort of under 20—ten is even better), and some people struggle with the lack of personal contact (or the temptation to multi-task during calls!).

Programs with structured peer relationships give you a great place to practice—if they have a good system and a way to assign compatible partners. And one-to-one instruction is a wonderful way to learn—just make sure you get an experienced trainer and the cost isn't out of sight. Which structure sounds best for you?

3. What kind of credential do you need for your target audience?

To this point, the standard bearer for credentialing is the International Coach Federation. But at the risk of being labeled a heretic, there are other choices. In corporate settings, an ICF credential is a must. However, a graduate degree program may be a better choice for coaching in academia. If you coach mainly in the ministry world, as I do, having an ICF credential is far down the list of what people look for in a coach—most people are completely unaware of it. It may also be that a certification in your key tools (like Strengths Finder or Myers-Briggs) will carry more weight with your target audience than your coaching credential.

This is not to say you shouldn't go through a rigorous training program. Anyone who wants to coach for a living should become certified. Just think through what you really need before you choose.

4. Do you share their values?

A coaching school is going to operate out of and train you in a fundamental set of values for how to influence people. I've talked to a lot of coaches who were very dissatisfied with the values conveyed in their training. Some eventually went to a second or even a third school in the search for one that was compatible with their world view, principles or spiritual values. Make sure you understand what values the school conveys before you sign on.

Application

How to decide which coaching certification program is the best fit for you.

Hints & Tips

What Can You Afford?

If you save a few thousand dollars on your coach training, but because of it blow two years unsuccessfully trying to start a coaching business, you're being penny-wise and pound-foolish. Think through how much of your success will depend on your training, and how much you are really putting at risk before you make price your number one criteria.

The Coaching Process

"Computers are useless.
They can only give you answers."

Pablo Picasso

One reason coaching conversations are powerful is that they bring structure to the process of thinking, planning, deciding and doing. Instead of just talking about your needs, you are systematically walking through a *framework* that forces you to clarify an objective, explore new options, make firm decisions and become accountable to act on your choices. That's a lot more than just talking!

Section II focuses on the basic asking skills that make up the framework of a coaching conversation: setting an agenda, defining the problem, creating goal statements, exploration, developing options, addressing obstacles and taking action. Mastery of these core disciplines is essential in almost any coaching conversation. Many of these sections contain more than one coaching tool, so you can learn multiple ways to tackle tasks like asking probing questions or helping the client develop potential solutions.

Conversational Models

Section II also presents two conversational models: GROW and the Coaching Funnel. A conversational model is a formal, step-by-step path through a coaching conversation. This is a great place for beginning coaches to start: you'll find that learning a conversational model makes it easier to stay focused through the coaching conversation and understand what your next steps should be. And removing some of your uncertainty about overall strategy helps you stay in the moment with the client instead of trying to plot out your next steps while they are talking.

If you feel a strong need to build skills in this area, the "Become a Master of Asking" exercise on page ten is a perfect place to start. It gives you a schedule of interactive exercises you can do with a friend or peer coach to develop your asking abilities.

Conversational Models

It's the client's job to decide on the agenda for a coaching interaction. The coach's role is to take that agenda and manage the conversation so that you arrive at the desired destination. The coach asks questions that help the client go deeper, think new thoughts and develop solutions, all the while keeping in mind where the conversation is going, how much time remains and what conversational threads need to be brought to closure. A key challenge for beginning coaches is learning to be mindful of these broader issues while remaining fully engaged in listening to the person you are coaching. When you are just starting out, that's a handful!

Conversational models can help. These predefined structures for a coaching conversation take you step-by-step from the agenda toward solutions and actions, while hitting all the key steps in between. Mastering one or two of these conversational structures helps you forward the conversation in an effective, intentional way without the distraction of having to figure out your next step on the fly.

A Model for Everything

Coaches have developed many different models for different applications. One of the best known models is GROW, a mnemonic which stands for Goal > Reality Check > Options > Will (see pg. 28-29). In this model, you first set a <u>G</u>oal for the coaching conversation. Then you identify an objective starting point for the change (the <u>R</u>eality Check), generate a number of potential courses of action (<u>O</u>ptions), and in the "<u>W</u>ill" step choose one or more options and convert them to committed actions. GROW works best for practical, performance-oriented issues like increasing job performance, getting organized or starting an exercise program.

The Coaching Funnel (see pg. 30-31) uses the visual image of two funnels joined at the mouth to describe a coaching conversation. In this model, the conversation starts with a narrow focus on a specific goal, broadens out as the situation and options for addressing it are explored, and then narrows back down again to specific steps of action. The Coaching Funnel puts more emphasis on exploration than models like GROW, so it works well for self-discovery issues, decision-making or processing what's going on in life.

Coaching Encounters

Conversational models are also perfect for coaching encounters—short, one-time coaching interactions. Because they make conversations more efficient and move intentionally toward action, these models can work well in conversations as short as ten minutes. And because conversational models use an easily explained step-by-step process, they are a great way to demonstrate and explain what you do to individuals who are unfamiliar with coaching.

Exercise: Conversational Models

Choose a conversational model and find five opportunities to practice it this week. In addition to formal coaching situations, you can use it to troubleshoot problems at work, with your kids or your spouse, in the hall after church—anywhere you are having a serious conversation you want to go somewhere. Then, try the same thing for a second week. Ten repetitions will put you well on your way to mastery.

Application

A look at formal structures for organizing the coaching conversation.

Hints & Tips

At first, choose just one conversational model and use it repeatedly until you can do it without thinking. Real competence with one tool leads to faster improvement than a partial grasp of several. The goal is not simply to know a model, but to master it. Then you can devote your full attention to being in the moment with the client.

For More

The GROW Model

The most widely used conversational structure in coaching is probably GROW (the acronym stands for <u>G</u>oal > <u>R</u>eality Check > <u>O</u>ptions > <u>W</u>ill). This four-step progression leads the coachee from defining an objective through clearly defining their starting point (the Reality Check), developing several potential courses of action (Options) and creating concrete action steps with high buy-in (Will) to actually move toward the goal. It's an excellent choice for helping people through practical issues like changing a habit or increasing performance, and it is also great for demonstrating the coaching approach to a prospective client in a short time.

The GROW model focuses on objectivity and concrete action, so it works best for getting practical things done. Outward goals like doing a project, forming a new habit or improving performance work best. Internal issues such as deciding what I really want in life or overcoming internal obstacles (which tend to be meandering journeys of self-discovery) often work better with a more free-form approach.

Goal

The goal is the objective the person wants to reach. In a one-time coaching encounter, it is what you will have accomplished by the end of the conversation, while in a coaching relationship you may work at a goal over many sessions. Make sure you have a clear, specific goal at the start: if the goal is vague, you'll have a hard time with the other steps in the GROW model.

Goal Questions
- *"What do you most want to talk about?"*
- *"What outcome would make this conversation a great success?"*
- *"What do you want to get out of our time together?"*
- *"How could you rephrase that goal so it depends only on what you do and not on others?"*

Long-Term Goal Questions
- *"What specifically do you want to accomplish?"*
- *"What will be different as a result of working on this area?"*
- *"How can we make that goal measurable—so we know when you've achieved it?"*
- *"By when do you want to have this done?"*
- *"In a month or three months—whatever time frame you want to work in—what do you want to have accomplished?"*

Reality Check

The function of the reality check is to determine an objective starting point for the desired change. You are attempting to ascertain the concrete facts of how things stand right now, as opposed to the person's subjective impressions of reality.

Reality Check Questions
- *"How many times did you do that in the last week?"*
- *"What is your weight (or monthly sales, or the state of your in-box) right now?"*
- *"When was the last time that happened?"*
- *"What have you actually accomplished on this today? How about this week?"*

- *"Who else is involved in the situation, and how?"*
- *"What have you tried already? What difference did those actions make?"*
- *"Which factors are most important in this matter?"*
- *"What events or choices led you to this place?"*

Options

The options step is process of thinking creatively to develop several potential solutions. Allow the client to do the hard work of thinking things through instead of making a lot of suggestions. See page 41 for a variety of additional techniques for generating options.

Option Questions
- *"What could you do about this?"*
- *"What other potential courses of action can you think of?"*
- *"Let's shoot for at least five potential solutions. What else could you do?"*
- *"If you had unlimited resources and knew you couldn't fail, what would you try?"*
- *"What if this obstacle was removed? What would you do then?"*
- *"What could you do to overcome this obstacle? What are your options?"*
- *"Who could help you?"*
- *"What other resources could you draw on to tackle this? Who else could you ask for creative ideas?"*
- *"What have you seen others do that might work for you?"*

Hints & Tips

Brainstorming options within the bounds of the resources you currently have limits potential solutions. Using hypothetical, "what if" questions to remove those limitations can be very empowering.

Will

This step is where you turn the preferred solution into concrete action steps with high buy-in. Ensure that you've created steps that will actually get done by looking for at least an "eight" on the first question under "Checking Motivation" below. For answers less than eight, troubleshoot obstacles or adjust the deadline of the step to increase the probability of a successful outcome.

Will Questions
- *"Which option(s) do you want to pursue?"*
- *"Turn that into an action step: what <u>will</u> you do by when?"*
- *"What step could you take this week that would move you toward your goal?"*
- *"You mentioned that you could do _____. What will you commit to doing?"*

Checking Motivation
- *"On a scale of one to ten, how likely is it that this step will get done in the time frame you've set?"*
- *"How could we alter that step to turn that 'six' into an 'eight'?"*
- *"Are there any obstacles we need to address to make sure this step gets done?"*

For More

The book *Coaching for Performance* by John Whitmore describes the GROW model in depth.

The Coaching Funnel

The Coaching Funnel is a visual model of a coaching conversation which allows ample time on the front end to explore the situation before generating options and actions. It starts with a narrowly focused goal: what is the person's ultimate objective? Then the coach widens the conversation with open questions that allow the person to more fully explore what's going on in the situation, both internally and externally. Getting more information out on the table helps the client generate potential solutions to the problem. Then the conversation begins to narrow again. The client evaluates these options and decides on a course of action. The coaching interaction concludes when the client chooses specific steps of action to move toward the goal.

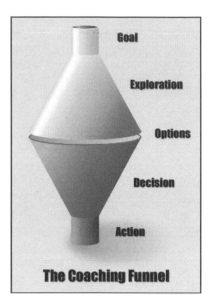

The Coaching Funnel

Step 1: Goal

The goal is a one-sentence statement of the objective the client wants to reach by a particular date. The S.M.A.R.T. format (pg. 37) is a useful tool for developing effective goal statements. Asking the client to state their objective in one short sentence is valuable: you can return repeatedly to a clear, succinct statement keeps you focused on the objective.

Goal Questions

- *"What do you want to accomplish through this coaching relationship?"*
- *"Be specific: what will be different when you've reached this goal?"*
- *"Can you think of a way to quantify that so we can measure your progress?"*
- *"In a month or three months or a year—whatever time frame you want to work in—what change do you want to have made?"*
- *"How can we state your objective so it depends only on what you do, and not on the choices or actions of others?"*
- *"Now take that and state it in one short sentence: what do you want to accomplish, by when?"*

Step 2: Exploration

Once a goal is set, it's time to fully explore the situation, what led up to it, and what is going on under the surface. Exploration can involve probing both the external situation and the client's internal responses to what is happening (see Probing Questions, pg. 41-43).

Exploration Questions

- *"Tell me more."*
- *"You mentioned that _____. Can you say more about that?"*
- *"Give me some background: what led up to your being in this situation?"*
- *"You mentioned that you always feel _____. Give me a specific example of a time that happened, including the details of what was said and done."*
- *"What's behind that?"*
- *"What are the most important factors or players in this situation?"*
- *"It sounds like _____ is really important to you. Can you explain?"*

Step 3: Options

In this step, the coaching process pushes the client to think creatively to develop multiple potential solutions. Often the first several ideas are ones that the person has already considered; the process becomes genuinely powerful when clients get creative and think beyond the boxes they are stuck in.

Option Questions
- *"What could you do here to move yourself toward your goal?"*
- *"What other options can you think of?"*
- *"Let's shoot for at least five potential solutions. What else could you do?"*
- *"You mentioned earlier that _____. Does that suggest any other ways you could approach this?"*
- *"What obstacles might keep you from reaching your goal? How could you remove them?"*
- *"What have you done in similar situations in the past?"*

Step 4: Decision

Next, help your clients make a decisive choice to pursue a certain course of action that leads toward their goal. A useful framework is "Could Do>Want to>Will Do" covered on page 44. Options are what coachees "Could Do". Next, ask for a decision on which potential solution they "Want To" pursue, then close the deal by requesting a commitment to what they "Will Do" to put their choice into action.

Decision Questions
- *"The options you mentioned are* [read back through the list of options the client has generated]. *What stands out to you in that list?"*
- *"Which options do you want to pursue?"*
- *"Which of these options will most effectively move you toward your goal?"*
- *"Make a choice: what's the best solution?"*

Step 5: Action

Now we'll turn the course of action the client has chosen into concrete steps with high buy-in. Clearly verbalizing what will be done creates both commitment and accountability.

Action Step Questions
- *"Let's turn that into an action step: what exactly will you do?"*
- *"What will you do by when?"*
- *"You mentioned that you (could, should, might, ought to) do _____. Would you like to make that into an action step?"*
- *"You mentioned that you could do _____. What will you commit to doing?"*
- *"Is that a realistic timetable? Are there any other obstacles we need to address before you move forward with this step?"*

The book *Leadership Coaching* by Tony Stoltzfus describes the Coaching Funnel in detail.

Hints & Tips

Details shared in the exploration step often suggest potential solutions. Returning to key things you noted during exploration can help the client generate additional options.

Hints & Tips

The solution the client believes in and wants to act on is usually the best option (even if you think you know a better one), simply because it will be acted on while other options will not.

For More

Application

How to help the client choose an agenda they're motivated to work on.

The Coaching Agenda

One of the first tasks in a coaching conversation is deciding what you are going to talk about. In coaching, the agenda comes from the client. A well-designed coaching agenda has four characteristics—use the acronym O.P.U.S. to help you remember them:

- **Ownership.** This is the person's own idea, s/he has bought into it and is committed to it.
- **Passion.** There is energy around this goal. The person is motivated to pursue it.
- **Urgency.** This isn't a someday thing: the person feels a strong need to act, now.
- **Significance.** This is important, will make a real difference, and is worth sacrificing for.

Looking Forward

- *"What do you most want to talk about today?"*
- *"What could we work on that would make the most difference for you?"*
- *"What's going on in life that's got your attention right now?"*
- *"What do you want more of in life? What do you want less of?"*
- *"If you got really radical today, stopped fearing the consequences and launched out to be what you were born to be, what would you be doing?"*
- *"How full is your tank—of love, of relationships, of fulfilling work, of spiritual life, of peace of mind? Where do you long for more?"*
- *"Tell me about a big dream that you've always wanted to go after."*
- *"What would be most helpful to focus on right now? It could be an upcoming decision, a practical challenge you face, a transition, a dream, you name it."*

Leaving Things Behind

- *"What is getting in the way of living the life you want?"*
- *"What do you lack?"*
- *"What do you most need that you don't have to live a life of passion and purpose?"*
- *"If one burden could be removed from you in the next 30 days, what would that be?"*
- *"If you could wave a magic wand and change any one thing about your life, what would that be? What led you to choose that?"*
- *"Where are you stuck or not moving forward? What is frustrating your progress?"*
- *"What area of life are you most motivated to improve?"*

Organizations and Leadership

- *"Where do you see your organization going in a year? What objective are you shooting for?"*
- *"What's the growing edge for you as a leader right now? For your organization?"*
- *"What brings you 80% of your joy in leadership? What's causing 80% of your stress?"*
- *"What three things do you most want to change in the next 90 days?"*
- *"What one thing do you need to focus on to take this organization to the next level?"*
- *"What stands in the way of you being the best in your market niche?"*
- *"Why did you take this job (or start this company)? What would it take for your dreams here to be achieved?"*
- *"What needs to change about who you are for your organization to go where it needs to go?"*
- *"What changes would make work an adventure again instead of a drudgery?"*

Hints & Tips

Coaching engagements often begin with a practical need ("I want to get control of my schedule"), then in a few sessions move to a deeper level ("I don't know what I'm living for"). Some clients won't disclose their true agenda until they feel they know you. And often it takes a coaching conversation to surface what they really want!

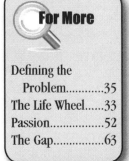

Life Wheel Assessment

Many coaches use assessments like a Life Wheel (see example below) to help clients determine what to work on. Ask the client to rank their satisfaction in each area of life, then discuss which area to focus on to increase their satisfaction.

- *"Rank your satisfaction with each of these areas of life from one to ten."*
- *"What stands out to you as you look at how you ranked these different areas?"*
- *"Talk about your two highest and your two lowest scores. What led you to give these answers?"*
- *"Which area are you most motivated to work on?"*
- *"Which area could we make the biggest difference with the least amount of effort?"*
- *"What led you to single out this category to work on?"*
- *"What would a "ten" look like in that area?"*
- *"What would it take to raise that 'six' to an 'eight'? How about to a 'ten'?"*

Application

A tool to help clients assess their lives and decide on an agenda for the coaching relationship.

The Eight Life Areas

The Life Wheel allows the client to self-assess in eight key areas:

- **Work:** Your career
- **Money:** Income, investments, retirement
- **Living Environment:** Your setting: home or apartment, office, car, etc.
- **Personal Growth:** What you do to learn or improve yourself
- **Health and Recreation:** Everything you do to take care of yourself
- **Community:** Friends, community involvement, social life
- **Family:** Married/single life, children
- **God:** Your spiritual life

Life Wheel Assessment

Hints & Tips

Create a personalized Life Wheel for your unique coaching niche by identifying six to ten areas your clients commonly work on and assessing their satisfaction with each area.

Using the Assessment

Once the assessment is filled out, use these questions to help the client unpack what is going on in a certain area and choose what to work on:

Work

- *"Be specific: what makes you satisfied/dissatisfied with your work?"*
- *"How does your real-world career path compare with what you expected it to be?"*
- *"What's most important to you in a job? How well does your current job supply that?"*
- *"What needs to change?"*

Money

- *"What led you to rank 'Money' as a _____?"*
- *"What do you care about in this area of life? What are your money values?"*

- *"Give me a quick overview of what is going on in your financial life. What's got your attention?"*
- *"What would you like to see change this year in your finances?"*

Living Environment

- *"How do the things you own enhance your life? And how do they detract from it?"*
- *"Name some 'things' (i.e. something you'd buy) you think would make you happy. Which ones will really make the most difference?"*
- *"What in your environment bothers you or drains your energy?"*
- *"If you could make one change in your living environment, what would it be?"*

Personal Growth

- *"What's the cutting edge for you right now in personal growth?"*
- *"What one new skill would make all the difference right now in reaching your dreams?"*
- *"What skills, attributes or areas of expertise do you want to develop this year?"*
- *"Where are you motivated to improve yourself or your abilities right now?"*

Health and Recreation (Self-Care)

- *"How's your health?"*
- *"What are you tolerating or coping with in this area?"*
- *"How satisfied are you with the kind and amount of rest and recreation you have in your life?"*
- *"Where do you need to take better care of your mind, emotions, or body?"*

Community

- *"Describe your social life for me. How satisfied are you with that?"*
- *"What do you most want in a friend? Where are those kind of people in your life?"*
- *"How do you want to be involved in your community? What's your contribution?"*
- *"Where are you serving others freely, just to give life away?"*

Family

- *"How do you experience your family/marriage right now?"*
- *"What's best about your marriage/family life? What would you most like to see change?"*
- *"Paint me a picture of what a great marriage or family life would look like to you."*
- *"What are you committed to in this area?"*

God

- *"Describe your relationship with God. What is it like?"*
- *"What do you aspire to in this area? What is your ideal?"*
- *"What is the gap? What's missing?"*
- *"How do you think God wants to meet you or relate to you?"*

Life Wheel Exercise

Copy the wheel chart, and have a friend, peer or family member fill it out. Then take ten minutes to help the person identify which area s/he is most motivated to work on by using some of the questions above.

For More

Defining the Problem

A key challenge at the start of a coaching relationship is helping the client identify the right problem to solve. For instance, you can spend a lot of time helping a person create systems to manage time and tasks, only to find that the client is constantly sabotaging the plan to meet a personal need or uphold an unspoken value that is hiding under the surface. How do you go beyond the surface to help center the coaching conversation on the real need? Below are several problem-defining questions, followed by three key areas to tune into that can take the conversation to a deeper level.

Application

Tools for getting beneath the surface to the real issue.

- *"What is the most important problem you want to solve?"*
- *"What would make a lasting difference and not just a temporary one?"*
- *"How does this connect with your overall objectives in life? With your values? Your dreams?"*
- *"What's behind this?"*
- *"If making this change was easy, you'd have done it already, and without my help. What makes it difficult?"*

One-Time Problem or Pattern?

Sometimes coaching goals go awry because you are dealing with a pattern and not just a one-time problem. For instance, busy people often convince themselves that if they just get through the latest project, their schedule will clear out. Is that reality or a pipe dream? A good way to find out is to explore the person's past experiences in this area of their life:

- *"What obstacles to change have you run into in the past in this area?"*
- *"In the last two years, how much of the time has this area of your life been working the way you want it to?"*
- *"Is this the first time you've dealt with this challenge, or have you faced it before?"*
- *"Step back and take an honest look at this area: is this a one-time issue for you, or something you struggle with a lot?"*
- *"What I'm hearing you say is that you can do this if you are just more disciplined. Be honest with yourself: has that worked for you here in the past?"*

Circumstance or Attitude?

It's a natural human instinct to want to change the externals (circumstances or the people around us). However, many times the solution lies in changing ourselves or our responses instead of changing our situation—particularly when we don't control what's going on around us.

- *"Do you need to change your situation, or change the way you respond to it?"*
- *"On a scale of one to ten, how would you rate your attitude in this situation?"*
- *"Is the best you coming across in this situation? What could you do differently to better align your responses with your values?"*
- *"What are your expectations in this situation? Are those expectations serving you well or frustrating you?"*
- *"So far I've heard you talk about what others need to change for things to get better. Just for the sake of argument, let's say they never change. What would you do then?"*
- *"What in this situation is within your control, that you can realistically change?"*

Hints & Tips

Working at change by just trying harder or being more committed is what I call a "brute force approach". Who we are hasn't changed, and we have no new ideas to try—we are just applying more brute force to the tools we already have. Patterns rarely yield to brute force: usually something deeper in us must change before the same disciplines that were ineffective before suddenly start working.

Symptom or Cure?

It's common for coaching clients to work on symptoms and not the cure. They want to create more family time in their life, when the real issue is an inability to say, "No," or that their identity is totally bound up in work. Coaching is transformational when it gets down below the symptoms to the problem itself. Here are two ways to do it:

1. Ask for more: pursue a **permanent cure** instead of a coping strategy:

  - *"What would it look like to conquer this once and for all?"*
  - *"What if you set out to remake yourself in such a way that you never had to discipline yourself in this area again—that living true to your values came as naturally as breathing? Take a few moments and envision that with me."*
  - *"What do you believe about your own ability to change in this area?"*

2. Explore **what drives the behavior** (where the energy behind it comes from):

  - *"You've told me what you do that you want to change—now let's explore the energy behind that. What causes you to function this way?"*
  - *"What do you gain from responding this way? What does it give you that you need?"*
  - *"Just as an exercise, let's imagine that you are handling this the way you are because you <u>choose</u> to do so. What's leading you to make that choice?"*

Defining the Problem Exercise

Find a place in your own life where you are stuck or stymied, something that comes hard for you, or where you've struggled following through on a change, and run that challenge through the three categories of questions above. Pick out some questions from each category and use them to evaluate whether this is a one-time problem or pattern; circumstance or attitude; and if you are working with the symptom or the cure. This is also a great exercise to do with a peer coach and work through with each other.

Hints & Tips

A change tool I often use is simply to try the easiest solution first, and see what happens. If a client believes s/he can change just by creating a some reminders or by setting up a practical structure, then go for it. If it works, that's great. If they hit a big obstacle instead, then you've found the heart of the problem—and that's great, too.

For More

SMART Goals

There are important advantages to coaching around a goal statement: a one-sentence declaration of a specific future objective the client has committed to reaching. For the coach, it's the mandate you coach the person toward. Without a goal, it is easy to divert the client to whatever you think the agenda should be. For the client, it is an important touchstone for staying focused.

The S.M.A.R.T. format (Specific, Measurable, Attainable, Relevant and Time-Specific) is one of the most widely used goal-setting tools. Walking through it as you set goals helps maintain the discipline of developing clear, timed, important and reachable objectives.

Specific: You can state clearly where you are going

- *"What exactly do you want to accomplish?"*
- *"What will it look like when you reach your objective?"*
- *"Choose a time frame that makes sense for this objective, and tell me exactly what you want to have accomplished by then."*
- *"Be more specific: what is the outcome that you want?"*

Measurable: You've included a way to measure progress

- *"How can you quantify this goal (put it into a number) so we'll know when you've reached it?"*
- *"You said you want a 'more balanced life': define what you mean by 'more.'"*
- *"How could you state this objective so your progress toward it is measurable?"*

Attainable: It is within your capabilities and depends only on you

- *"Is this goal within your capabilities? Is it reasonably possible?"*
- *"Are there any barriers or circumstances that preclude reaching this goal?"*
- *"Does this goal depend on anyone else's choices? How can we reword it so it depends only on you?"*

Relevant: You care enough about this goal to make it a priority

- *"Why is this important to you?"*
- *"What are you willing to let go of or cut from your schedule to work on this goal?"*
- *"On a scale of one to ten, how important is it to you to reach this goal?"*

Time-Specific: It has a deadline

- *"By when will you reach the goal? (Or by when will this be an established habit)?"*
- *"When will you start?"*
- *"What's your deadline?"*

Application

A tool for quickly creating effective goal statements.

Hints & Tips

A goal states the destination: the *where* and *when*, not the *how* (that's the action plan). The key to developing goal statements quickly is to stay focused **only** on where the client wants to go, and to avoid talking about how to get there until after the goal is set.

For More

Defining the
   Problem............35
Life Wheel............33
Organizational
   Coaching............85
Book Coaching.....88

Probing Questions

Application

Tools for asking exploratory questions that help the client think more deeply about a situation.

Probing questions are used in the initial stages of a coaching conversation to explore the client's situation. Probing gets more information out on the table and forces the coachee to really examine what is going on. Many times, just the act of exploring and thinking things through in a structured way will bring the solution, without even looking at options.

Open questions are the key to effective exploration. They can be defined in two ways:

- A question that can't be answered with a simple "yes" or "no"
- A question that lets the coachee answer in many different ways and thereby direct the conversation to what's most important

Broad Questions

The second definition is of most interest to coaches. Coaches use many wide open questions because we want to be led by the coachee's sense of what is important, not our own. A "Broad" question that can be answered in many different ways lets the coachee take you to what is most significant. It's a little counter-intuitive if you are used to being led by your own insights, but asking broad questions is a very efficient way to move the conversation onto the key agenda.

So what do broad questions look like? For instance, take the example of coaching someone through a disagreement at work. Which of the following two queries is broadest?

- *"What did you say in reply?"*
- *"How did you respond?"*

The second option is better (unless you specifically want to know what was said), because it allows for many more types of responses. It may be that the person voiced a "nice" reply, but then sulked for a week, or updated his resume, or coldly plotted how to get revenge. Or it could be that he said nothing, but chose to respond with an act of kindness or loyalty. The point is, *the most significant response may not have been in words*. Because the first question limits the answers to what was said, it may prevent the client from telling you what's really important. We tend to ask narrow questions like this one when we ask with a solution already in mind.

Exercise: Broaden Your Questions

To make a question broader, redesign it to allow for a wider range of answers. Here's an example, plus four more narrow questions for you to practice broadening:

1. *"Describe that feeling of disappointment."* (Narrow)
   "Describe that feeling." (Broader: allows for many different emotions)
   "Describe what was going on in you." (Even broader: allows for emotions plus physical, rational or other types of responses)

2. *"Who could you ask to find the answer?"*
3. *"Which of these two subjects would you like to focus on?"*
4. *"What's the most significant thing that happened to you today?"*
5. *"How is what's going on at home connected to your stress at work?"*

Playing the Angles

Another important probing skill is looking at a situation from multiple angles. Pursuing different sources of information (like the Past, Others' Viewpoints, or Emotion) brings new insights and opens up additional solutions when you get to the "options" stage of the conversation. Here are several different angles you might choose to explore, with sample questions for each:

The Past
- *"What led up to this?"*
- *"Give me some background: how did you arrive at this place?"*
- *"What else fed into this?"*

The Future
- *"Where do you see this going?"*
- *"How do you want things to turn out? What's the best possible outcome?"*
- *"What's the dream or the compelling future that calls you on here?"*

Patterns
- *"Have you been in a place like this before? Describe what happened."*
- *"How have similar situations in the past affected you? How have you responded to them?"*
- *"Do you see any patterns here in your life or your responses?"*

Emotions
- *"What is going on inside you during this change?"*
- *"How do you feel about that?"*
- *"Describe the emotions this situation brings to the surface in you."*

Others' Viewpoints
- *"How do you think your* [boss, spouse, peers, etc.] *see this?"*
- *"What does this look like from the other person's point of view?"*
- *"If you were _____, what would things look like from that person's perspective?"*

The Concrete
- *"Give me a specific example of that."*
- *"What exactly did you say? What did she say?"*
- *"OK—so run through that from square one. Exactly what happened?"*

Values and Principles
- *"What values do you hold that will influence your responses to this?"*
- *"What principles* [business, ethical, spiritual, etc.] *apply to this situation?"*
- *"What would it mean to be true to your beliefs and principles in this situation?"*

The Heart of the Matter
- *"What are the real issues here?"*
- *"What makes this significant to you?"*
- *"It seems like this is something important to you—talk about that a little."*

Hints & Tips

During coach training, many prospective coaches find that their previous pattern has been to quickly enter into problem-solving mode—often within 60 seconds of beginning a conversation. A wonderful discipline when you're learning to coach is to commit to probe and listen for at least five minutes before you even begin examining solutions. You'll be surprised at how much more effectively you coach!

Probing (cont'd)

Short and Sweet

Sometimes the best question is the simplest. Here are some very simple queries that are used repeatedly in coaching situations. If you can't think of what to ask, fall back on one of these basic coaching questions.

- *"Say more about that."*
- *"Keep going."*
- *"Tell me more."*
- *"What else?"*
- *"And?"*
- *"What's behind that?"*
- *"You mentioned that _____* [Insert a phrase that caught your attention]. *Tell me more about that. "*(The Observation and Question technique.)

Twelve General Probing Questions

Here are twelve questions you'll use over and over as you coach:

1. *"What would you like to talk about today?"*
2. *"What else is important to this discussion?"*
3. *"What feelings do you have about this?"*
4. *"Who are the other players in this? How are they involved?"*
5. *"What do you want? What's the objective here?"*
6. *"What do you gain from this? What do you give to it?"*
7. *"Give me a concrete example of that."*
8. *"What did you mean when you said _____?"'*
9. *"What was most significant to you about that situation?"*
10. *"Give me some background: what led up to this situation?"*
11. *"What excites you about this? What holds you back?"*
12. *"What is your heart saying?"*

For More

Conversation
    Starters............18
Exploration..........30
Top Ten Asking
    Mistakes...........12

Observation and Question Exercise

Here's an exercise to help you become comfortable with simple questions and break out of the need to ask the perfect question. We're going to do a whole ten-minute exploratory conversation using just the observation and question technique (the last item under "Short and Sweet" above). Once the conversation gets started, simply listen for the most significant or interesting thing the person says, repeat that phrase back, and ask, "Tell me more about that." It's amazing how deep you can go if you get yourself out of the way, listen intently and keep asking a simple probing question!

Options

Generating options by asking the coachee to think instead of offering advice or solutions is one of the most important coaching skills. Below are five techniques for developing options.

The Five Options Technique

When we are mulling over a challenge we face on our own, we tend to stop thinking creatively after two or three options. If those options don't look very attractive, we get stuck. The Five Options Technique gets people unstuck by pushing them beyond that initial set of options and back into the creative zone. Simply ask for at least five potential solutions to the problem, and keep asking until you get five.

- *"Give me five options for how you could tackle this challenge."*
- *"Give me another option."*
- *"What else could you do?"*
- *"If you got really radical, what would you try?"*
- *"OK. The options you mentioned so far are* [list them]. *Which of these would you like to pursue?"*

Make sure the clients are doing the work! Your job is to push them to think things farther through than they have before, not to do the thinking for them. If the coachee runs out of new ideas, begin asking more specific questions using the clues in what they've said:

- *"What have you done in the past in similar situations?"*
- *"You mentioned talking with your spouse as an option. Who else could you bring into this?"*
- *"How could you kill two birds with one stone here, or fit this into what you are already doing?"*
- *"All the options you mentioned involve you doing this by yourself. If you thought outside that box, what else could you do?"*

Obstacle Approach

This approach starts with the barriers the client has run up against. Identify what's standing in the way of achieving the goal, and develop options to move around it.

- *"What is stopping you from reaching that objective?"*
- *"What do you need that you don't have to reach this goal?"*
- *"You've mentioned money several times as an obstacle. If you had all the money you needed, then what would you do?"*
- *"I've heard you say twice that you don't have time to take this on. Let's look at that obstacle: give me five options for how you could find the time."* [See the *Five Options Technique* above.]
- *"How could you change your objectives or timetable to make this goal achievable?"*
- *"What resources could you tap into to overcome this obstacle?"*
- *"Who do you know that could help you with this?"*
- *"How have you overcome obstacles like this in similar situations in the past?"*

Application

These asking tools provide a variety of ways to help the coachee develop creative solutions— a vital step in the coaching process.

Hints & Tips

Sometimes after all this the person will go back and choose the very first option they voiced. That's not a failure! The value of going through the whole process is now they really **believe** it's the best option, and so it is more likely to get done.

For More

Options (cont'd)

Ideal Future Technique

This technique asks the client to conceptualize their ideal future or the best possible outcome, and then work backward to the present. When we start in the present we often get stuck, because all we see are obstacles like time and money. Going to the future and working directly with the dream takes us out of this trap. By visualizing and experiencing our desired future, we often also gain the motivation needed to overcome the obstacles to reaching it.

Step 1: Identify a Goal or dream

- *"Where would you like to be with this in three to six months?"*
- *"What is the best possible outcome you can envision?"*
- *"Would you like to explore this dream and see if it is a real possibility?"*

Step 2: Go to the End. Take the person to a point in the future when the goal has come to pass

- *"Imagine that it is 90 days (or six months, or a year) in the future, and you've achieved this goal. Take me there and tell me about it."*
- *"Let's say you pursue this dream and you reach it—it becomes a reality. Take me to that point in the future and describe what it looks like to have reached this dream."*
- *"If you pursued this dream (or this solution or this decision), what would your life look like in 30 days (or 90 days or a year or five years)?"*

Step 3: Visualize the Ideal. Ask the person to picture their ideal future in detail!

- *"Imagine you are in that future right now. Envision it in specific detail! What do you see and feel?"*
- *"Visualize your typical day in this new future. What will your surroundings be like? Your schedule? Your team? The work you are doing? What are you enjoying?"*
- *"Be more specific. What kind of setting are you in? Where are you sitting? Who are you meeting with? What are you talking about?"*
- *"What does it mean to you to reach this goal? What difference does it make?"*
- *"Paint me a picture: what emotions would you experience if you reached this goal?"*

Step 4: Work Backward to the present to develop a solution

- *"Where is your motivation to pursue this goal now, versus half an hour ago?"*
- *"What difference does that make as you consider the obstacles to reaching this goal?"*
- *"What one step could you take now to start moving toward your ideal future?"*

Transformational Approach

Sometimes the best solution comes through transforming who you are (your attitudes, expectations, or responses) instead of changing your outward circumstances. These questions explore the possibility of inward transformation to bring about outward change:

- *"What could change about **you** that would change your situation?"*
- *"Let's assume for a minute that this situation is custom designed for your inner growth as a leader and a person. If that's true, what's the opportunity here?"*

- *"When we face great adversity, we are either broken by it, survive it, or it becomes a defining moment. What response would make this a defining moment for you?"*
- *"What fears, doubts or other internal obstacles are keeping you from moving forward? What would it take for those obstacles to be completely gone?"*
- *"Imagine that at age 75 you are telling your life story to a grandchild. What would you like to be able to tell him/her about how you responded to this challenge?"*
- *"If you were the best you can be, operating at your full potential, the person you've always wanted to become—then what would you do?"*
- *"If this situation wasn't random adversity, but a gift from God, what then?"*

Thinking Outside the Box

Sometimes coachees get stuck inside a box—all their potential solutions fall within certain unrecognized boundaries. For instance, the person may only look at options they think will fit in their busy schedule or limited budget, or they may unconsciously believe they can't be happy unless some *other* person changes. When you see a coachee functioning inside a box, name the box, then help them explore what might happen if they went outside it. A box might be:

The other person must change for things to get better:

- *"Envision yourself as a change agent here—that your response makes a real difference. If you saw yourself as powerful instead of powerless, what would you do?"*
- *"Just for the sake of argument, let's say the other person never changes. Can you live with that? Then what could you do to make things better?"*

The resources I have now are the only ones available:

- *"Get creative: what other resources could you tap into?"*
- *"The solutions I've heard so far are limited by the resources you have now. What could you do to broaden the resources you could throw at this?"*

There is some external circumstance I'm stuck with and can't change:

- *"I'm noticing that all your options assume you have to stay in this [job, home, relationship, role, schedule, etc]. Can I challenge that? What if you made a more fundamental change?"*
- *"What if your schedule or budget wasn't a given? If you had more time and money, what other options would you have?"*

There is something about myself that I can't change:

- *"What would you do if you really believed in yourself and knew you couldn't fail?"*
- *"It seems like you are assuming that _____ can't change. Is that really true?"*

There is a belief or principle that I hold to that can't change:

- *"What belief or principle are you functioning out of here? Is that belief serving you well or hindering you? What do you want to do about that?"*
- *"Your options seem to be shaped by a belief that _____. Does that belief work here? Could reevaluating or adjusting it lead to some better options?"*

Hints & Tips

One way to identify a box is that solutions occur to you that don't occur to the coachee. Instead of just telling them your ideas, it may be much more powerful to help them think about why that idea wasn't occurring to them. When you figure out how this idea breaks the box, the coachee may immediately think of several more answers.

Application

Tools for creating effective steps and ensuring high buy-in throughout the process.

Action Steps

Could Do>Want To> Will Do Model

The end result of a coaching conversation is a set of action steps that create tangible progress toward the goal. If you aren't creating actions, you aren't coaching. When converting options into action steps, move from possibilities to decisions to committed actions using this model.

- **Could Do:** Option questions explore possibilities (i.e., "What else *could you do*?").
- **Want To:** Ask the client to choose an option ("Which option do you *want to* pursue?").
- **Will Do:** Ask for commitment to a specific step ("Tell me exactly what you *will do*, by when.")

"Could Do" lets the client explore before committing. By asking for a decision first (in the "Want To" step, you gain permission to nail the person down to a concrete action. "Will Do" elicits commitment. Using all three steps ensures high buy-in.

Hints & Tips

While the first part of the coaching conversation uses lots of open questions, you'll need to move toward direct questions to help the coachee make a firm decision to pursue a specific action step.

- *"What could you do?"* [options]
- *"Which of these options do you want to pursue?"*
- *"Is that a step you want to take?"*
- *"Make that into an action step: what exactly are you going to do?"*
- *"What will you do, by when?"*
- *"What will you commit to do in the next two weeks to keep moving forward?"*
- *"What's your next step?"*

Could Do>Want To> Will Do Exercise

With your peer coach, start with a practical problem, develop some options using the Five Options Technique (see pg. 41), and coach each other through to at least two action steps, intentionally using the "Could Do>Want To>Will Do" framework. What do you observe about the function of the "Want To" step? What happens if you leave it out?

Insurance

Action steps that don't get done are worse than no steps at all—they sap confidence and energy, and make it less likely that future steps will succeed. As a coach, you want to encourage people to create doable steps with a high likelihood of success. If you are sensing that some extra insurance is needed to get a certain step done, try a question like one of these:

- *"Are there any obstacles to getting this done that we need to address?"*
- *"Who else do you need to check with or work with to make this happen?"*
- *"On a scale of one to ten, how confident are you that you'll complete the step by the deadline?"*
- *"What would it take to raise that 'seven' to an 'eight' or 'nine?'"*
- *"How could you change the step or the deadline to make it more realistic?"*
- *"What could you do to increase your chances of getting this done successfully?"*
- *"Do you need any accountability on this?"*

Equivocation

Equivocal language is a tip-off that the coachee has not fully committed to a course of action. At right are some examples of equivocation. Use the coaching questions below to get past it.

- *"Are you ready to commit to that step?"*
- *"You mentioned that you 'might' take that step. Is anything holding you back?"*
- *"You are saying you 'ought to' do this. What would make it into something you'll do because you really want to do it?"*
- *"You're waffling. You can choose to do this or not do it—I just need to hear a clear decision one way or the other. What will you do?"*
- *"Is there anything we need to change or discuss about the step that would help you make a decisive choice on this?"*

The Four Tests of an Action Step (CD²)

Effective action steps have these four characteristics:

- **Clarity:** I know exactly what to do
- **Datebook:** This step can be scheduled at a specific time
- **Commitment:** I know I *will* do this
- **Deadline:** I've set a date for completion

Progress Report Guidelines

Many coaches ask for a progress report (either written or verbal) at the beginning of each new session to establish some accountability for prior steps. Asking one question and letting the client respond (instead of ticking down through the action items in your own notes) forces the client to keep a list of steps and be ready to report on them—a good discipline. Here are four guidelines for an effective verbal progress report.

1. Do it first thing in your appointment, so you don't run out of time and omit it.
2. Use the client's action step list, not yours.
3. Ask the client to touch on all action steps. Come back later to ones that need follow-up.
4. Be brief: use three to five minutes, so you don't use up the whole session with reporting.

Progress Report Questions

- *"Give me a brief progress report on your action steps."*
- *"Give me a quick update on what you've accomplished since we last met."*

Exercise: The Four Tests of an Action Step

Look back on the action steps you've recorded from your last few coaching sessions. Do you have clear steps for each client? How well do those steps fit the four tests of an action step (CD²—see above)? If there is a particular characteristic that your steps don't seem to fit, how can you be intentional about changing that in future coaching sessions?

Hints & Tips

Here are some typical examples of equivocal language: to be on the look-out for when you are creating action steps:

"I could..."
"I might..."
"I'm thinking of..."
"Maybe I should..."
"I ought to..."
"I'd like to..."
"If..."
"Someday..."
"One possibility.."

For More

Options...............41
Obstacles.............46
Accountability.......73
Decisions.............70
Getting
  Organized..........87

Identifying Obstacles

Obstacles are what make simple things hard to do. When a client approaches you to make a practical change, often the real need is addressing the hidden obstacles that thwart progress. For example, if the goal is getting control of one's schedule, the real issue may be standing up to others' demands and saying, "no!"; or completing what seem to be a boring responsibility instead of chasing the excitement of a new dream; or admitting that you are addicted to work. Change is rarely as simple as it looks on the surface. It is helpful to remember: "If it was easy, you'd have done it already."

Obstacles can be practical, external factors, like time and money; or internal barriers such as fears, beliefs or needs. Below are questions for surfacing these different types of obstacles:

Identifying External Obstacles

- *"What is stopping you?"*
- *"What makes this hard to get done?"*
- *"What do you need that you don't have to reach your objective?"*
- *"What external factors will your plan have to account for if it is going to work?"*
- *"When you've tried to make changes like this in the past, what got in the way?"*
- *"Is there one key obstacle here—that if you conquered that one thing it would make a decisive difference in reaching this goal?"*
- *"What one resource or tool would make all the difference if you had it?"*

Identifying Internal Obstacles

- *"What goes on inside you when you think of launching into this? Feel free to name an emotion, a physical sensation, a memory, anything."*
- *"Relax for a minute, and pay attention to what's going on in you. Where do you feel pressure or strain or stress around this idea/situation?"*
- *"You've found it hard to make this change. What do you gain from not changing?"*
- *"What would you lose that's important to you if you did change?"*
- *"What's your worst-case scenario here? What's the fear behind that?"*
- *"What's driving your responses?"*
- *"What belief is behind your responses? How well is that belief serving you?"*
- *"What's the critical voice in you saying about this situation?"*

For More

Identifying Obstacles Exercise

Ask a friend or your peer coach to allow you to coach him/her for 15 to 20 minutes on a place in life s/he is stuck or stymied. What's something your friend has been thinking about for some time but hasn't acted on, or can't figure out what to do with? (Areas s/he is tolerating, conflict situations or difficult changes can be fruitful areas to look.) Now, coach the person toward an action step in this area, using some of the questions above. What obstacles came to the surface? How did you discover them? What did your friend learn about him/herself through this process?

To follow up, try the exercise under "Overcoming Obstacles" (pg. 48).

Overcoming Obstacles: Seven Strategies

1. Dream Without It

Imagine that the obstacle is gone, and ask the person to dream without it. Experiencing the possibility that the dream could happen can provide enough energy to tackle the obstacle.

Application

Seven practical techniques for overcoming obstacles, with sample questions for each.

- *"Let's just remove that obstacle from the equation for a minute—imagine it is all taken care of. How does that change things? How do you feel about pursuing this dream now?"*
- *"If you had unlimited resources and couldn't fail, what would you do then?"*
- *"What if you **did** have the money (or time, or resources)? Then what?"*

2. Find What Worked in the Past

Different change strategies work for different people. A great way to find something that works for you is to explore what you did in similar situations in the past. The act of reflecting on past successes builds courage and confidence as well as bringing to mind practical solutions.

- *"When you've faced this kind of obstacle in the past, how did you overcome it?"*
- *"Tell me about a time when you faced into a fear and beat it. How'd you do it?"*
- *"Think back to a few months ago when we were working on ____. What was the turning point for you there? From that success, what can you apply to this challenge?"*

3. Brainstorm Options

Use any of the options techniques (see pg. 41-43) to find ways around an external obstacle.

- *"Give me five options for how you could overcome that obstacle."*
- *"What resources do you need to conquer this obstacle? Where could you get them?"*

4. Walk in the Light

Internal obstacles have the most power over us when they live in the darkness, unexamined and not understood. When we bring them out into the light, name them and talk about them with others, they lose much of their aura of invincibility.

- *"Can you name what you are afraid of? What's the thing you don't want to happen?"*
- *"What's your worst-case scenario? What makes that the worst for you?"*
- *"What goes on inside you when you attempt to tackle this? Can you describe it?"*

5. Stir Up the Darkness

Sometimes the veil around an internal obstacle is thick enough that coachees can't name the obstacle—they know they've hit a wall, but they don't know how or what or why. One way to gain new information on the obstacle is to stir up the darkness: intentionally do the thing you are afraid of (in a small dose) and track what happens inside you as you do it. Here's a request you might make of a coaching client:

- *"I'd like to make a request. This week, find a small way to do the thing you fear, then sit down for 20 minutes immediately afterward and journal about it to discover what's going on in you. Jot down what happened, what emotions you experienced, and any physical sensations you had (i.e. you got a knot in your stomach). Doing this will help surface the internal obstacle."*

6. Use Hypotheticals

Sometimes obstacles are intractable because we can't imagine living without them. We may cling to a risk aversion that we think protects us but actually causes great loss, or hang onto a response pattern that helped us cope in childhood but doesn't work at the office. It can be hard to even contemplate letting go of a deep-seated belief or an important safeguard. One way to help a client over this barrier is with Hypotheticals. Hypotheticals are imaginary scenarios that let us play with new ideas or beliefs without committing ourselves to embrace them. Here are several examples of how to use Hypotheticals in coaching situations:

- *"The belief I'm hearing here is that you have to save everything in case there's a rainy day. Imagine for a minute that we can see into the future, and nothing is going to happen that will eat into your financial reserves for the next five years. How would that change the way you'd live?"*
- *"I hear you saying that you're going to get stuck with all the follow-up on this project because nobody else cares. Let's play with that idea for a minute. What are some other possibilities? See if you can give me three other reasonable scenarios for why the details don't seem to get done."*
- *"So you don't want to get close to people and then, two years later, have to move away and leave your friends. That makes sense. But try this on: what if you knew that those friendships would actually get richer and deeper after you moved? How would that change things for you?"* [If it would, then you can explore how you might maintain friendships at a distance.]

7. Find the Reason

People have a good reason for what they do. Even if a belief or behavior seems irrational on the surface, it makes sense within the rationality of the person who chose it. If you can find the reason, and bring it to the surface, you can often change the behavior.

- *"What led you to respond in that way? Walk me through the reasoning behind it."*
- *"So you are saying that conflict is a no-win situation, and so you avoid it. Can you identify where that belief comes from? Where'd you learn to see conflict that way?"*
- *"It seems like you are sabotaging yourself—you get close to winning and then you do something that snatches defeat from the jaws of victory. What's going on there?"*

Hints & Tips

The best Hypotheticals are ones that challenge the belief in a plausible way. Before you pose one, take a few moments and think through how to make it one that the person can identify with. Can you draw a parallel with some other area of the person's life, equate this area with another that they do well at, or pose it in the familiar terms of work or family? The more the person can enter into the scenario, the more they'll learn.

For More

Tackling Obstacles Exercise

Do the "Identifying Obstacles" exercise on page 46 with your peer coach. Once you've each come up with an obstacle or two, coach each other through several of these seven techniques. Then take ten minutes or so and debrief. What worked? Why did it work? What did you learn?

Life Coaching and Destiny Discovery

Life coaching tends to focus in on two things: identifying and pursuing your life purpose, and refocusing your present life for greater energy, fulfillment, and productivity. In other words, creating a better future *and* a better life today.

A problem on the better future side is that we coaches throw around a lot of similar terms (destiny, life purpose, calling, passion, design) without really nailing down what they mean. Here are some life purpose terms defined in a way we can use when working with destiny discovery:

- **Design:** My innate traits, my "Nature": talents, personality type, learning style, etc. I have a sense of destiny when I work at roles or tasks that are closely aligned with my design.
- **Experience:** The wisdom, learned skills, and other assets I acquire along the way in life that I leverage toward my life purpose. The "Nurture" counterpoint to Design's "Nature".
- **Destiny:** The future I am innately designed for *and* prepared for by my experiences.
- **Passion:** The internal energy I have to pursue something I care deeply about.
- **Calling**: An external commission I accept to serve a greater good. My impetus/choice to serve certain others without regard to personal reward.
- **Fulfillment:** A lasting sense of joy and satisfaction from living out my life purpose.

Clarifying the meaning of these terms leads to an overall definition for life purpose:

> ### Life Purpose
> The energy of <u>Passion</u>, channeled through my <u>Experience</u> and <u>Design</u> in the service of a greater <u>Calling</u>. Pursuing one's life purpose generates lasting <u>fulfillment</u> and significance.

This definition contains the idea that living a life of purpose is much more than the pursuit of personal happiness or fulfillment. Test that statement for yourself: in your experience, are people you know (or people you see in the public arena) who pursue recognition, money, power or pleasure as an ultimate end really happy when they attain it? Or when they are asked, "How much is enough?" do they answer like John Rockefeller (one of the world's richest men at the time): "Just a little bit more?" Paradoxically, fulfillment pursued as an end in itself is a dead end.

Understanding Fulfillment

So what is fulfillment? It includes positive things like joy, success, peace of mind, pleasure and recognition. But often the most fulfilling things in life are ones that we've suffered for (one of the meanings of the word "passion" has to do with suffering), things we've sacrificed to attain (like training hard to play at a championship level), or things that are more about making others happy than they are about serving ourselves. In fact, the positive emotions of fulfillment tend to come most strongly as a result of hard work and sacrifice in service of an end that is bigger than just me.

There *are* times to focus on making a person happier. When a client is stuck in a frustrating job, a relationship with no boundaries or a self-defeating belief, simply helping them move out of those difficult circumstances can be a great thing. But if the road to lasting fulfillment passes through pain as well as pleasure, that cannot be the only way we coach. Would we ask an NFL star why he tolerates the pain of all those workouts? No!—because that pain leads him to his purpose. Helping the client embrace suffering, find meaning in pain, or even discover a life calling in that difficult experience may do far more to create the *lasting* fulfillment of living in your purpose than simply finding what is making them uncomfortable and removing it from their life.

Design: Who Am I?

Everyone has things they already know about who they are and what they are made to do (even though some people don't yet know what they know). From roles that fit or didn't fit you, to experiences of passion and fulfillment or an inner knowing of what you're made for, many life purpose clues are already present. A key role the coach plays is helping the coachee consciously identify these cues and assemble them into an overall picture.

Inner Knowing

That grounded inner sense of who you really are.

- *"What do you know already about what you were made to do?"*
- *"What's been most meaningful to you in life? Where have you found real purpose in living?"*
- *"When you were a kid, what did you want to be when you grew up? What roles attracted you?"*
- *"Sometimes we have a deep, intuitive sense of what we want to do or be in life, without even knowing exactly where it came from. What would fall in that category for you?"*

Roles

Examining how past roles fit or didn't fit provides important clues to one's design.

- *"What kinds of roles or responsibilities do you enjoy and feel good at? What sucks you dry?"*
- *"Of all the roles you've been in, which ones were the best fit? Why?"*
- *"Which roles have been the worst fit? What do you know **isn't** part of your ideal role or ideal life?"*
- *"Name three specific things that would definitely be part of your best job (or role)—and three things that definitely wouldn't!"*

Experiences

Your life experience uniquely prepares you for something: what is it?

- *"If every experience of your life was planned to train you for your destiny, what would you say your whole life has prepared you to do?"*
- *"What experiences have you had that gave you an unusual sense of purpose? Describe them."*
- *"What has your life experience told you about your destiny?"*
- *"What valuable experiences can you draw on to accomplish your dreams?"*

Affirmation/Feedback

When you are moving in your purpose, people around you will often recognize and affirm it.

- *"What do those who know you well say about what you are made to do?"*
- *"When have you been greatly affirmed in who you are and what you're born for?"*
- *"What have you done that has been the most successful or beneficial to others?"*
- *"What relationships or people have influenced your sense of destiny? How?"*

Coaching Questions: A Coach's Guide to Powerful Asking Skills

Personality Assessment

These assessments are designed to help identify and name parts of your design.

- *"Do you know your personality type from DiSC, Myers-Briggs, Strengths-Finder or some other instrument? What have you learned from it about who you are?"*
- *"How would a good friend describe what you are like? Which of your traits seem to stand out to others?"*
- *"What are your most outstanding personality traits?"*

Strengths and Weaknesses

Many people can name things they are good at; fewer have connected strengths and destiny.

- *"What are you great at? What are your best talents or natural abilities?"*
- *"What are you most effective at? Where do you have the most impact?"*
- *"What are at least five of your key strengths? How about three weaknesses?"*
- *"What do others who know you well say that you are good at or not good at?"*

Revelation

Ninety-some percent of Americans believe in God. Many report a sense of revelation or experience of divine disclosure connected with their sense of destiny.

- *"What do you feel has been revealed to you about your own destiny or call?"*
- *"What is your sense of God's unique purpose for your life?"*
- *"Have you had an experience where it felt like God showed you something about your destiny? Tell me about it."*
- *"What part does your relationship with God play in your sense of life purpose?"*

Family

The family, community and culture you are born into can have a significant impact on your personal sense of destiny.

- *"Is there a sense of call or destiny that was passed down to you from your parents?"*
- *"Can you name any sense of purpose that runs through your family? What kinds of groups, causes or missions do members of your family tend to get involved with?"*
- *"What is your family's historical legacy? How do/don't you want to be part of that?"*
- *"What sense of purpose have your drawn from your culture or community?"*

Client Exercise: Life Purpose Inventory

Answer the questions from each category above to create a life purpose inventory: a summary of what you already know about your life purpose. This is a great base-line exercise to do at the start of a destiny discovery process—it makes it easy for the client to see measurable progress in understanding their design.

Hints & Tips

Understanding your personality type is vital to identifying and living out your destiny. Personality instruments like DiSC and Myers-Briggs are among the most powerful, well-accepted self-discovery tools available. Becoming certified to administer and interpret one of these instruments is an excellent way to increase your credibility and add value to your coaching clients.

For More

Experience...........58
Ideal Life/Role......55
Affirmation...........69
Reflection.............80
Career Coaching...86

Application

Four areas that can be explored to identify a person's core passion.

Passion: What Motivates Me?

Here are four areas to probe to help identify a person's deepest motivations.

Passion

- *"What are you most passionate about in life?"*
- *"If you had a year to live, what would be most important to you to do and be in that time?"*
- *"What makes your heart sing?"*
- *"What do you do that would be hardest to do without?"*
- *"What are the places in life or roles you fill that most touch your own emotions— where you find yourself laughing, crying, joyful, sad, discouraged or inspired?"*
- *"What really gets your goat? What are the issues, injustices, principles or causes that you get riled up about?"*

Quotes...

"Some men see things as they are and say, 'Why?' I dream of things that never were and say, 'Why not?'"

George Bernard Shaw

Energy

- *"What are three things you've done that you couldn't wait to get at each day? How about three things you dreaded and constantly wanted to avoid?"*
- *"What are some things in life that you have a lot of energy for? Why those things? And where does the energy for them come from?"*
- *"When was the time in life where you had the most (or least) energy? What were you doing in those times that energized or de-energized you?"*
- *"What do you see around you that you want to fight for (or against)? What are you willing to pay a price for?"*

Fulfillment

- *"What's been the most satisfying thing you've done? What made it so fulfilling?"*
- *"What in life gives you lasting satisfaction?"*
- *"What have you done that you are most proud of?"*
- *"What accomplishment or legacy would have ultimate significance for you?"*
- *"What have you done in life that you'd love to do more of?"*
- *"What makes you feel fully alive when you are doing it? What have you done that gives you the feeling of being right in the sweet spot of life?"*

Changing the World

- *"If you could invest the rest of your life and know you could change one thing in the world around you, what would it be? What led you to choose that?"*
- *"What issues do you truly care about in the world around you?"*
- *"What needs have you encountered in life that you'd jump at the chance to meet on a larger scale?"*
- *"Have you ever seen a tragedy on the news that made you cry? What was it? Why did it impact you that way?"*
- *"What is the need (or the people) whose cry touches the depths of your heart?"*
- *"Imagine yourself at the end of your life looking back. Is there a dream in you of serving or helping others that would cause you deep regret if you never took the risk to go for it?"*

For More

Dreams and Desires

Dreams are potential future objectives that attract us. It's the stuff we want to do, but (unlike goals) we haven't committed ourselves or planned to reach them yet. Dreaming is a great way to uncover what people really want in life. These questions can all be used as reflection exercises.

Getting Started

- *"Take the eight life areas [Work, Money, Living Environment, Personal Growth, Health and Recreation, Community, Family, God—see page 33] and list some dreams for each."*
- *"What would you like to do in your life? Your dreams can be large or small, significant or for fun, for others or for you. What do you dream of doing?"*

Big Dreams

- *"Name some of your bigger dreams—what do you want to do that seems farther off or will take a while?"*
- *"If you had unlimited resources and couldn't fail, what would you set out to do?"*
- *"Is there a dream that you are afraid to voice, maybe for fear you'll look arrogant, or presumptuous, or you won't be able to do it?"*
- *"Dream bigger! What would that dream look like if you used your full capacity?"*
- *"If you dreamed in terms of your potential instead of your current capabilities, how would it change this dream?"*

"Fun" Dreams

Fun dreams are things we want to do just to learn, for fun, or to say we've done them. These smaller dreams offer clues to our larger purpose by showing what we love and are drawn to.

- *"What experiences do you want to have in your lifetime?"*
- *"What do you want to learn? What skills do you want to master?"*
- *"What are ten things you'd like to do in life purely for the fun of it?"*
- *"Where would you like to go in your life? What would you like to see and do?"*
- *"What do you want to build or create in your lifetime, just for the joy of creativity?"*

Regrets

- *"Imagine you are 80 years old and looking back at your life. Which dream from your list would cause the greatest regret if you had NOT pursued it?"*
- *"You've voiced the cost of pursuing this dream. What's the cost of NOT pursuing it?"*
- *"Let's say you basically stay on your current career/life path until the day you retire. If you were looking back on that life, how would you feel about it?"*
- *"What will you lose if you just stay safe, stay here, and don't chase your dreams?"*

Client Exercise: Dream Inventory

Use several of the questions above to create a list of dreams to pursue before you die. Give the person permission to be free and jot down whatever is on his/her heart or comes to mind: these are dreams that *could* happen, not goals that must be pursued!

Application

Ways to help others verbalize their dreams and enjoy the process.

Client Exercise: "Fun" Dream List

Request that the coachee create a Dream List of things s/he wants to do or experience in life just for the fun of it. Then examine the list together. What clues do you see to the person's larger life purpose? What connections do you see to bigger dreams s/he has expressed? How many of these dreams can be realized in a year? In three? In ten?

For More

Dream Barriers

Occasionally one of your clients will hit a dream barrier: an obstacle to freely looking at the future. Here are some questions to ask when you hit a barrier:

- *"What is stopping you from dreaming freely?"*
- *"It seems like you are limiting yourself. Can you name the barrier? What would it look like if you took that limitation off of your dreams?"*
- *"This approach seems to be difficult for you: let's see if we can find a dreaming style that fits you better. Think of a dream you had or a time you were dreaming freely in the past. How did you come up with those dreams?"*

Fears

Common dream barriers are fear of failure, fear of success (expectations will be even higher next time), fear of commitment (because it limits future options), fear of looking bad, etc. One way to overcome fears is to make the dreaming process hypothetical. Instead of talking about what you want to or will pursue, talk about what you might pursue, or what you could do someday. Taking commitment out of the equation keeps people from locking up in performance fears.

- *"Let's dream about what you* might *want in the future. It doesn't matter if it never happens, or if you get everything right—let's just play around with some options."*
- *"Dreams are things you think about doing but you aren't committed to—in fact, you may never commit to doing them. Tell me some things that you'd like to think about doing."*
- *"Let's try something different: let's say that for this day only, anything you dream will come out good—there's no way that you can fail. If that were true, what would you dream about?"*
- *"You have permission today to dream without worrying about how things will turn out. Assume that you'll make the right adjustments along the way, and everything will work out. So given that, what would you like to do or be someday?"*

Dreaming for Non-Dreamers

Some personality types are not wired for picturing a hypothetical future that is disconnected from the present. The people we think of as dreamers (who are 'N's on the Myers-Briggs assessment) live in the world of ideas, and can create an ideal future out of nothing. But those who are 'S's on the MBTI (half the population) are pragmatic dreamers. They live in the present, and tend to only envision a future that can practically be extrapolated from the present. They are often frustrated by traditional dreaming exercises.

The key to helping practical people dream is to identify what they've loved doing in the past (or what they are doing now that they love), and help them envision ways they can *do more of that* in the future. This provides the practical connection to reality they need to dream effectively.

- *"What have you done in the past that's been truly satisfying? How could you do more of that?"*
- *"What do you like/dislike about your current role? What kind of role would maximize the likes and minimize the dislikes?"*
- *"In what kind of situations (or with which people) have you been most effective or had the greatest impact? How could you reorient life to spend more time there?"*

Quotes...

"Whatever you can do, or dream you can, begin it. Boldness has genius, power and magic in it. Begin it now."

Goethe

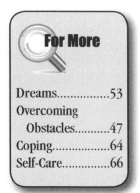

Ideal Life

Creating a picture of an ideal life is an oft-used coaching exercise. By clearly identifying the ideal and comparing it with reality, we can identify the gaps (see pg. 63) that need to be bridged to reach a better future. This gap between the real and the ideal is often where the client finds the motivation to leave what is secure and known and to make major life changes.

Ideal Life

- *"Take the eight major life areas [Work, Money, Living Environment, Personal Growth, Health and Recreation, Community, Family, God] and sketch out what your ideal life would look like in each area."*
- *"Visualize yourself at a time in the future when you are living your ideal life. How would that look?"*
- *"Imagine you are in your ideal home environment. Describe the setting: the rooms, décor, location, the things you have around you. What would be just right for you?"*
- *"What kind of relationships would you want in your ideal life? What would your family, friends, marriage or single life look like?"*
- *"Draw me a picture of an ideal day. What would you be doing throughout it?"*
- *"Go into more detail. For instance, you mentioned daily exercise. What do you do for exercise, where are you doing it, and who do you interact with along the way?"*
- *"What kind of lifestyle have you dreamed of in the past that you've laid aside as silly or impractical? Those images can contain clues to what's really important to you—would you be willing to share some of those dreams with me?"*

Ideal Role

- *"Create a job description that is a perfect fit for who you are."*
- *"What would make your ideal job significant or fulfilling to you?"*
- *"What kind of career might be a great fit for your passion, experience and abilities? Flesh that out—what would that role look like?"*
- *"In your ideal job, what would you do yourself and what would you delegate? What would you be responsible for, and what would others handle?"*
- *"Name five things you'd be doing in an ideal role, and five things you wouldn't do."*
- *"Who would you be working with in your ideal role?"*
- *"What's your ideal weekly schedule? How would you arrange your tasks to best fit your natural rhythms?"*
- *"Imagine you are working in an organization that's a perfect fit for you. What would the organizational culture and values be?"*

Ideal Team

- *"Visualize your ideal team. Who would be on it? What would each person do?"*
- *"What would your role be on this ideal team?"*
- *"What would be your team's mission?"*
- *"What skills or personality types do you need on your team to complement yours?"*
- *"What three characteristics or values are most important to you in a fellow team member?"*
- *"Describe the corporate culture or relational climate of your ideal team. What would those relationships be like?*

Application

Designing an ideal life helps people get in touch with what they most want.

Client Exercise: Find Your Ideal

Have the coachee pick several questions from these lists to reflect on his/her ideal life, role or team. Emphasize the need to create a detailed, visual picture of the ideal—can the person draw a picture s/he can really live in, touch, taste and experience?

For More

Application

Tools for under-standing and iden-tifying values, and refining them into value statements.

Values

Values are the bedrock of behavior. They define what is most important to us, they form the framework we use for making decisions, and they are the driving force behind our work and our passions. But because they are such deeply ingrained assumptions, we're often not consciously aware of what they are or how they shape our actions. Values discovery can be a powerful tool to help clients get in touch with who they are.

Values Discovery Questions

- *"What are some of your core values?"*
- *"What things, if they were taken away or you couldn't do them, would make life unbearable? What makes these things valuable to you?"*
- *"When making your most important decisions, what are the fundamentals you base them on?"*
- *"Where do you invest the best of your time, money and energy? Why?"*
- *"What are your 'soap box' issues? Your deep concerns? Why?"*
- *"What do you take the most pride in? What most excites you in life? Why?"*

Values Characteristics

One effective way to refine value statements is to make sure they fit the definition of a value. Here are several characteristics of values with questions for each:

Values Are Passionate
- *"What are the things in this area that you care most deeply about?"*
- *"Let's find the heart of this. What parts would you be most willing to sacrifice for?"*
- *"What's behind that? What makes you passionate about it?"*

Values Are Unique
- *"The language you are using could be true of a lot of people. Can you say that in a way that captures what is unique about you?"*
- *"_____ is a fairly generic phrase. Can you personalize that a little more?"*
- *"Can you say that in a way that if your friends read it, they'd know it was you?"*

Values Are Lived (Not just something you aspire to)
- *"How well is this statement reflected in your life right now?"*
- *"Show me how you are living out this value in practical ways right now."*
- *"Is that a value that you are living out already, or is it something you aspire to that we might set a goal to reach for?"*

Values Are Concise
- *"Now, can you sum that up in one sentence?"*
- *"Can you shorten that into some pithy, meaningful phrases that can be unpacked?"*

Values Tool: The Eight Categories

The biggest challenge with values is that getting hold of them is like nailing jello to the wall. One way to make the process easier to grasp is to use a framework like the Eight Life Areas (Work, Money, Living Environment, Personal Growth, Health and Recreation, Community, Family, God—see page 33). Ask coachees to do a values brain-dump of words and phrases that describe what

Exercise: Refining Value Statements

The end point of a values identification process is creating a set of five to ten one-sentence value statements that sum up the client's most deeply held values. Usually you'll start with some jotted notes and then convert them to formal statements.

A great way to refine these initial jottings is to keep asking, "And why is that important to you?" When the person starts repeating back the same answers, you've probably gotten to the bottom of the value.

they care most about in each category. The key to the brain-dump is to resist trying to organize or evaluate your thoughts—just start writing what comes to mind for five minutes or so in each area. Once you've finished, take the brain dump and refine it further using the exercise on page 56.

Values Exercise: Word Choice

Another way to work at values discovery is to allow the client to choose from a list of descriptive words, and then create value statements from those words.

- *"Which of these words resonate most with you? Pick no more than ten."*
- *"Which words represent what you care about most or the ideas you live by?"*
- *"Pick out five or six words from the list below that describe what is most important to you in each of the eight life areas."*

Integrity	Freedom	Relationship	Financial independence
Honesty	Exploration	Team	Stewardship
Genuineness	Creativity	Community	Frugality
Authenticity	Fun	Belonging	Overflow
Accountability	Artistic	Depth	Sharing
Do what you say	Spontaneity	Being known	Benevolence
Directness	Flexibility	Intimacy	Life-long learning
Sincerity	Knowledge	Commitment	Investment
Strength	Identity	Friendship	Success
Character	The search	Communication	Recognition
Follow-through	Meaning	Gentleness	Community involvement
Sacrifice	Influence	Compassion	Career advancement
Legacy	Truth	Caring	Efficiency
Family	Passion	Emotion	Accomplishment
Marriage	Seeing the world	Spiritual life	Focus
Duty	Adventure	Health	Purpose
Honor	Diversity	Devotion	Achievement
Heritage	Travel	Passionate pursuit	Building
Responsibility	Change	Worship	Leadership
Harmony	Movement	Generosity	Mastery
Security	New challenges	Service	Competence
Stability	Opportunity	Reflection	Precision
Peace	Enthusiasm	Reaching out	Excellence
Home	Starting things	Evangelism	Doing it well
Thoughtfulness	Entrepreneurial	Changing the world	Planning
Practicality	Motivation	Hospitality	Being knowledgeable
Nurture	Progress	Concern	Principles
Love	Inspiration	Integration	Rationality
Beauty	Renewal	Making a difference	Nature
Romance	Healing	Volunteering	The outdoors

Hints & Tips

Two books of interest to coaches that have in-depth information on understanding and developing a value set are *The Path* by Laurie Beth Jones, and *Values Driven Leadership*, by Aubrey Malphurs

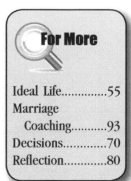

For More

Experience: Life's Prep School

Experience is the third area that must be tapped to fully grasp one's life purpose. And here, there is no such thing as a wasted life. Every experience, good or bad, can be leveraged into a person's sense of destiny. The key to finding meaning in pain or difficulty is understanding that every experience is a *qualification*. Success is the experiential qualification we identify most readily—for instance, you succeed at your position and that qualifies you for promotion.

- *"What has your whole life prepared you to do?"*
- *"What experiences have most shaped who you are as a person? How have those changes prepared you for what you most want to do in life?"*
- *"Don't just think work—combine all your experiences, from all areas of life. What kind of role or task would bring all the best of what you've learned in life to bear?"*

Failures

A less-recognized idea is that failure (especially when followed with redemption) is a qualification as well. For instance, which experience would best qualify a person to start a placement program for prison inmates: a life where you've never had a run in with the law, or one where you screwed up, went to prison, and then put your life back together again? Certainly, the ex-offenders would find the second person most credible.

- *"At their point of need, people are most open to being influenced by someone who's gone through what they have. Given that, who has your life prepared you to serve?"*
- *"What have your failures and missteps qualified you to do?"*
- *"What opportunities might your mistakes open to you that wouldn't have come had you succeeded?"*
- *"What gifts have your failures given you?"*

Work Experience

- *"What knowledge or skills have you acquired in your career that you want to incorporate as you pursue your purpose in life?"*
- *"What have you accomplished in your career that you are most proud of?"*
- *"Name five work experiences that have readied you for your destiny. How have they prepared you to do what you're born to do?"*
- *"What are the five most important skills you'll need to fully live out your life purpose? On a scale of one to ten, what is your level of competency in each one? What does that tell you about where you are in your life purpose journey?"*
- *"If you were hiring yourself, what job would your experience best qualify you for?"*

Skills and Abilities

- *"What are some of your key learned skills?"*
- *"Name your top five skills and abilities, in terms of how useful they are to you."*
- *"What kinds of things are people always asking you to do for them? (In other words, which of your skills do others consistently recognize as valuable?")*
- *"What can you do, or do in a unique way, that almost no one else can?"*
- *"Give me two or three examples of skills you've picked up that have made a big difference in the trajectory of your life."*

Application

Questions that tap into your life experience to shed light on your life purpose.

Hints & Tips

Nurture and nature (Experience and Design) both influence who you are, and living one's purpose means putting all of yourself into what you do. The energy of *Passion*, channeled through one's *Experience* and *Design* in the service of a greater *Calling*, is the source of lasting fulfillment.

For More

Destiny Experiences Exercise

A *Destiny Experience* is a specific event where you felt totally in the zone: you were doing what you were born to do. These experiences point directly to our life purpose. The key to identifying them is to think of a *specific, discrete event or experience*: something that happened one day, over a weekend, or in a certain conversation. A Destiny Experience is NOT a role or an extended period in life where you felt fulfilled, but a specific event.

To examine Destiny Experiences, have the coachee use the list of questions below to think of three experiences that stand out (preferably from different seasons in life). Often destiny moments are marked by external confirmation—you succeeded at something important, you made a genuine difference, or others recognized and affirmed your ability.

- *"Give me an example of a time in your life—a specific day or single experience—where you felt like you were doing what you were born to do?"*
- *"Describe an experience where you felt fully alive, you were firing on all cylinders, and it seemed like everything you'd done in life equipped you for that moment."*

Part II

Take ten to fifteen minutes to examine each experience together, and identify as many specific details as you can remember about it using questions like the ones below. While you are listening, be alert to connections between those details and the person's life purpose. If this experience were a peek at the person's destiny, what do you see of the larger picture through this snap-shot?

- *"Exactly what happened? Walk me through the experience, step by step."*
- *"Who did you serve?"*
- *"What kind of task were you doing? How did you do it?"*
- *"How did you get into that situation?"*
- *"What was the impact of what you did on others?"*
- *"What was accomplished?"*
- *"What else can you remember?"*

Part III

Now, here's the fun part. Compare your three Destiny Experiences using the following questions. The key to this step is believing, since we sorted out stories with a high sense of destiny, that the details are all meaningful (especially when they pop up in more than one story). It is amazing what the specifics of these stories can tell us about what we were born to do.

- *"When you look at these three stories together, what stands out to you? What do they have in common?"*
- *"Which details of these stories were crucial to your impact or fulfillment in it?"*
- *"It seems that in each of your three stories, you _____ [served this certain kind of people, did this kind of task, experienced fulfillment through this result, etc.] What's going on there?"*
- *"It was interesting to me that _____ [cite a detail that caught your attention]. Is that an example of the way you were made to function? How does this connect to your life purpose?"*
- *"What led you to choose these stories instead of some others? What makes this story seem significant to you?"*

Application

How to mine the meaning from the special Destiny Experiences that point directly toward one's life purpose.

Example

One client cited an experience (as a 22-year-old army private) when he'd had the moxie to ask his colonel for funding to start a homeless relief project using army resources. It's an amazingly prescient event: now, he has great favor with people in authority, and regularly approaches them for resources to serve the less fortunate.

For More

Application

Tools for discovering one's calling to serve or give to others.

Quotes...

"I don't know what your destiny will be, but one thing I do know: the ones among you who will be really happy are those who have sought and found how to serve."

Albert
Schweitzer

Client Exercise: My Dying Day

Write your own obituary. What would you like your legacy to be? Your significant accomplishments? Whose life would be better because of your influence, and how? What character qualities would you most like to be remembered for?

Calling: Serving the Greater Good

For a variety of reasons, calling seems to be the least understood and tapped facet of life purpose. Calling is a commission coming from outside of your self, to serve something bigger than yourself. An important part of fulfillment is the sense of being part of something bigger than you are, of leaving a legacy, of making a difference for others or knowing that the world is a better place because of what you gave. Calling keeps life purpose from becoming narcissistic and selfish, while it addresses our deep desire to give our lives to something of lasting worth and significance.

Some individuals find a sense of call in being drawn to meet a specific societal need. One common pattern is the individual who has suffered difficulty or injustice finding their calling through fighting that injustice or alleviating that pain for others. Many find their call through their relationship with God, when they sense that God has commissioned them to serve others in a particular way for the good of all. Others find a commission to work for the greater good from their nation, company, family or community.

There is wide variation in how people experience a sense of call. It comes to the young and old, through pain or joy, urging us to give in huge, collective efforts or small, individual acts of kindness. While calling usually aligns with a person's passion and design, the fact that it comes from an external source makes it less predictable and not as easily found by searching within.

Legacy/Service

- *"What legacy do you want to leave behind? How will the world be a better place because you lived?"*
- *"What's a really great legacy look like to you? Give me an example or two of a life you truly admire."*
- *"What do you care most about that is bigger than you? It can be a cause, a goal, a principle, a people, a truth—what do you want to give your life to?"*
- *"What world-changing dream makes your heart beat faster?"*
- *"What form will your legacy take? Will it be people you've invested in, building an organization, something you've created, your family heritage—or what?"*
- *"If you could spend your life working to change one thing in the world that would make a real difference for others, what would that one thing be?"*
- *"Imagine you are at the end of your life looking back. What deeds would enable you to honestly say, 'That was a life well lived!'"*

Who Will You Serve?

One of the clearest clues to your calling is in the people or needs you consistently feel drawn to and reach out to serve. Identifying this "target audience" for your calling is very illuminating.

- *"Who do you want to help in your life? What kinds of people would you most like to make a difference for?"*
- *"Think back over the last 90 days. Who have you gone out of your way to help, in big ways or small? What drew you to each of those people?"*
- *"What needs do you see on the street, in people or on the news that grip your heart?"*
- *"What kind of injustice makes you want to ride to the rescue? What suffering are you most sensitized to?"*
- *"What causes fire you up? It could be the environment, adoption, digging wells in Africa, making your neighborhood safe, anything. What cause gets you angry,*

passionate, determined or excited?"

- *"In what areas do you repeatedly find others looking to you for hope, wisdom, service, or a touch of love? How does it touch your heart when they come to you?"*
- *"What groups do you serve or help with unusual impact?"*

Client Exercise: Who Will I Serve?

Take 45 minutes with the questions above to create a list of the individuals, groups, causes, needs, injustices, or bigger dreams that draw you to serve and give for the greater good. For each item on the list, ask yourself these three questions:

- *"Why am I drawn to this?"*
- *"How was I drawn to this?"*
- *"Why me? What do I bring to this?"*

Service from Suffering

Many people find a sense of call in their own suffering: they care deeply about helping those who are suffering in the same way they did. It's a fruitful area to probe for a sense of call.

- *"What individuals, groups or needs do you deeply identify with out of your own suffering? How do you want to help them?"*
- *"What difficulties have you faced that became defining moments when you overcame them? How have those experiences equipped you to serve others?"*
- *"Where in life have you been most deeply hurt? How could you turn that energy toward helping others in similar straits?"*
- *"What experiences of suffering or injustice have deeply marked you? How are you drawn to work with others in any of these areas?"*
- *"In what areas of your life that were broken or messed up in the past are you now helping others? What messages of hope does your life embody for others?"*

Tuning Into God

Being commissioned by your Creator engenders a powerful sense of destiny in people of faith. While there are well-known cases of those who manipulate us with God-talk to serve their own desires (Adolf Hitler comes to mind), they are greatly outnumbered by the anonymous heroes who have genuinely given and served out of their relationship with God.

- *"What do your spiritual values have to say about the purpose of life?"*
- *"What has God put you on this earth for? What are you made to do for others?"*
- *"Have you found a sense of call through your relationship with God? What is it?"*
- *"What could you do with the life you've been given that would make you look forward to showing the results to your Creator?"*
- *"What do you feel God has shown you about the unique purpose of your life?"*
- *"What has God spoken to you directly or through others about your calling?"*

Exercise: Finding Purpose in Suffering

See how many examples you can think of of people whose sense of purpose in life came through something they suffered, or was targeted at keeping others from suffering as they had. For instance, MADD (Mothers Against Drunk Driving) was founded by a woman whose child was killed by a drunk driver. Another example is Charles Colson, a Nixon aide who went to prison and out of that experience started a variety of programs to meet the needs of inmates.

For More

Life Coaching: A Better Life Today

"A plan in the heart of a man is like deep water,
but a man of understanding draws it out."

King Solomon

The other side of life coaching is creating a better life today. Here, the focus is on rearranging circumstances and attitudes in everyday life to discover increased joy and effectiveness while lowering stress and wasted energy.

The Gap

The process often starts by identifying "Gaps"—the places where real life falls short of your ideal—and making changes to close them. You can start from either side of the gap: either by identifying the person's ideal (see also *Ideal Life* on pg. 55) and then finding ways to move toward it; or by identifying What's Missing (the exercise on pg. 63) and figuring out how to either get it or make your peace with it. A great way to identify a gap is to help the client tune into what they are tolerating or coping with in life—use the exercises and examples on pages 64 and 65.

Another type of Gap is life balance. Juggling several important priorities (family, marriage, work, health) is a fact of life. When these commitments get out of balance or fail to reflect our most important values, we experience that as a gap. Great coaches help people become conscious of their underlying values (see pg. 56) and reapply them to everyday life to establish priorities. Consciously living out of your personal values is often experienced by the client as a great step forward in joy and purpose.

Self-Care

Self-care (pg. 66) is the practice of making it a priority to take care of yourself. The idea is that you can only love others well to the degree you love yourself. While taking care of yourself has been taken to unhelpful extremes in some coaching circles (lasting fulfillment tends to be bound up in serving a greater good and not just ones' own interests), the fact remains that many of us are not very good stewards of our own physical, emotional or spiritual health because we don't recognize the need to make it a priority. Coaches can help by observing how the client exercises self-care, reflecting this back to the client, and challenging self-destructive beliefs and attitudes.

Setting boundaries is simply exercising healthy self-care in relationships. Often the largest obstacle to a better life is the inability to say "no," or being driven to please others at any expense, or simply operating in muddled relationships where appropriate boundaries have never been defined.

In all these areas, the life coach works to help the client experience a better life today.

The Gap: What's Missing?

When you are coaching for a better life today, the process often centers around identifying and closing what coaches call "the gap". The gap is the distance between your needs and expectations and the way life is now. Another way of thinking about it is in terms of alignment: the gap is the place where your day-to-day life fails to align with your values and your life purpose.

- *"What is missing from your life right now?"*
- *"Take a look at some of the different areas of your life (family, work, home, finances, etc.) Where are you most satisfied? Where are you most dissatisfied?"*
- *"On a scale of one to ten, what's your stress level like right now? What would it be like if your stress was a quarter of that?"*
- *"Let's take a few minutes and explore your feelings about life. Imagine yourself at work—picture your office and the people there. What emotions bubble to the surface? How about when you visualize yourself at home? Looking at your finances? In your relationships?"*
- *"What percentage of your time do you feel like you are living in alignment with your calling right now? What would you like that number to be?"*
- *"Think about your true capacity—when you are in the right environment, well rested, fully engaged. What percentage of that capacity are you living right now?"*
- *"What are three things you love about your life? Three things that aren't ideal but you tolerate or put up with? How about three that really frustrate you?"*

Client Exercise: Take it or Leave it

This exercise examines how your real life aligns with your ideal. It is especially helpful if you aren't a natural dreamer because it extrapolates the ideal from past experience.

Make three columns on a piece of paper. The first is "Take It": these are the things you love and value about your life that you'd like more of in the future. The last column is "Leave It": these are things in your life that you dislike, drain you or crowd out what's important, that you'd like to leave behind. The middle column is "Take It or Leave It"—things you have no strong feelings about.

Use these follow-up questions to explore the "Take It or Leave It" exercise:

- *"When you look over your lists, what stands out?"*
- *"How does your life now align with your ideal? Where is there a good match, and where are things out of alignment?"*
- *"How well does your daily lifestyle support your life purpose? Where does it help, and where does it get in the way?"*
- *"What one thing on the "Leave It" list would make the most difference if you changed it?"*
- *"What here must change? What can you no longer tolerate?"*
- *"What step could you take now to better align daily life with your purpose?"*
- *"What would it take to deal with your entire "Leave It" list? What stops you from doing that?"*

Application

Questions for helping identify the gap between a person's expectations and reality.

Hints & Tips

The *Life Wheel Assessment* on page 33 is an excellent tool for identifying gaps, because it measures the coachee's satisfaction (or dissatisfaction) with different areas of life.

For More

Tolerating/Coping

We all have moments when we discover we've been tolerating something that is less than the best—when if we had taken the time to tune into it, we'd have changed it for the better. The questions below help us surface things we are tolerating. They can also be used as reflection questions for discussion with your family, spouse or team:

- *"Name three little annoyances in life that steal your energy or rob your joy."*
- *"What are you tolerating in your life? What are you putting up with that maybe you haven't even thought about taking action on until now?"*
- *"What are you putting up with in relationships? Name any conflicts, boundary issues, or problem situations that you're coping with instead of resolving."*
- *"Close your eyes and imagine walking through your house, room by room. What in each room do you want to avoid? What needs or unfinished tasks do you see? What rooms are energizing or enjoyable, and which give you negative feelings?"*
- *"What possessions that you no longer need are cluttering up your life?"*
- *"What worries clutter up your mind that you could let go of today?"*
- *"Does it feel like life is happening to you is this area? What proactive step could change that?"*
- *"What are the little quirks that you react to over and over in your relationships? What are your quirks that bother your friends?"*
- *"Where do the petty arguments with those you care about most get started? What unresolved hurts or past injustices are you carrying around with you that open the door to conflict?"*

Quotes...

"If you are pleased with what you are, you have stopped already. If you say, 'It is enough,' you are lost. Keep on walking, moving forward, trying for the goal."

St. Augustine

Client Exercise: Energy Drains

Use several of the questions above to create a list of energy drains: the little things in life you are putting up with that sap your energy. It may help to keep a list on your desk, so you can jot down things you're tolerating as you experience them; or you might want to take ten minutes each evening to review the day and tune in to what is bothering you.

At the end of the week, choose three energy drainers to eliminate, and create a strategy to either change your circumstances to remove them, or change your perspective to embrace them.

Dealing with Energy Drains

- *"It sounds to me like you are tolerating something there that you don't like. What could you do if you set out to take care of it once and for all?"*
- *"I've heard you describe some ways you could cope with this better. How about if you give me three ways you could conquer this instead of cope with it?"*
- *"What difference would it make in your life if this energy drain was gone?"*
- *"What one step could you take to de-clutter your environment, your mind, or your relationships that would most bring you peace?"*

Accepting What You Can't Change

In his book, *The Power of Purpose*, Peter Temes advances the idea that when we experience difficulty, the Western response is to change our external circumstances, while the Eastern mindset is to alter our inner attitudes and responses to make peace with those circumstances. Here are some questions that focus on changing inner attitudes instead of external circumstances:

- *"What would need to change in your attitudes or responses for you to function at your best in the midst of this, even if the circumstances don't change?"*
- *"If this circumstance is hard to get rid of or is beyond your control, how can you choose to experience it differently?"*
- *"If you can't change this, how can you make your peace with it?"*
- *"What is this experience teaching you? What is the gift this pain brings?"*
- *"What good could come of this? How could this teach you compassion, or grace, or endurance, or character?"*
- *"Research on survivors found that we are either broken by suffering, survive it and get life back to normal, or it becomes a defining moment in our lives. How could this experience become a defining moment for you, where you rise up and engage it out of what you were made to be?"*

Moving in the Opposite Spirit

One way of working at changing an attitude or character trait you don't like about yourself is to intentionally do the opposite. These questions are examples of how you might help your clients identify practical, simple steps they can take to move away from unhealthy life patterns:

- **Life feels like drudgery**. *"What are ten simple things you can do that would give you joy? Pick one or two and tell me how you could do more of that."*
- **I'm a self-centered person.** *"What are ten things you could do in the next 30 days to bless or serve those around you? "* Or, *"Pick five people, and ask each one to name something someone else did for them in the last few months that made their day. Then see how many of those ideas you can implement in the next month."*
- **I feel tired.** *"What are five things that feed your soul? How could you add more of these things to your schedule?"*
- **I'm frustrated with my team.** *"Let's see if we can turn that around. What are two great qualities of each of your teammates? Can I challenge you to find ways to publicly affirm those qualities in each teammate this month?"*

Coaching Exercise: Toleration

Get together with your peer coach to look at the area of toleration. Here's the challenge: as you coach your partner, can you help him or her identify at least five tolerations or energy drains? How about ten?

Then take one or more of the things you are tolerating and help each other develop concrete action steps to decisively deal with them, once and for all.

Hints & Tips

Sometimes we grow used to coping with our foibles—we see them as personality quirks, weaknesses, or "Just the way I am." Clients who believe this way will create coping strategies (ways to live with the thing), instead of genuine change strategies. If you sense your client coping, challenge it: *"What if, instead of coping with this thing, you dealt with it once and for all? What would your life look like if this was totally gone?"*

For More

Getting
   Organized..........87
Transformational
   Coaching...........94
Wellness
   Coaching..........89
Relationship
   Coaching...........90

Self-Care

If lasting fulfillment and significance comes from expanding your world by loving and serving others, one starting place is asking, "What do I have to give?" In this fast-paced, driven culture, often the answer is, "Not much." When your best energy goes toward surviving, there isn't much left for thriving, let alone giving. So often a first step in pursuing your calling is figuring out how to love yourself well.

Stress and Pace

- *"On a scale of one to ten, where is your stress level right now?"*
- *"When was the last time your stress was significantly lower? What changed?"*
- *"What would it be like if you were still experiencing this kind of stress a year from now? How about three years?"*
- *"Let's try to get in touch with what your emotions are saying to you. Pull out your datebook or your task list and let your feelings surface as you scan it. What emotions bubble up?"*
- *"What is your body saying about your pace? Are you ready to face each day, or is it tough to roll out of bed? What physical signs do you need to pay attention to?"*
- *"What are the people close to you saying about your pace or your schedule? What do you think they'd like you to hear?"*
- *"What do you gain from living an adrenalin-fueled lifestyle? What is driving you that causes you to keep choosing this pace and this stress level?"*

Making a Change of Pace

- *"What would your ideal pace look like? Describe a day or week lived at this pace."*
- *"What smaller changes could you make immediately to free up time and energy to tackle the bigger challenges you face?"*
- *"What one change would make the biggest difference in your stress level?"*
- *"If you set out to cut your stress by 80%, what would you do?"*
- *"Let's take a look at process: how do things that aren't priority end up on your schedule? Can you give me a few examples?"*

Life Balance and Priorities

We all juggle many task and responsibilities—that's what makes life balance a key coaching area. Priorities are an important part of developing a balanced life, as they separate the important from the urgent and help us divide our energy in a logical way to get the important things done.

- *"What led you to want to focus on life balance now? What makes this a priority?"*
- *"On a scale of one to ten, how do you feel about your life balance right now?"*
- *"What high-priority area of life is working best? Which most needs more attention?"*
- *"What low-priority area of life is stealing the most time and energy from you?"*
- *"It sounds like this has been nagging at you for some time, but you haven't been able to find the energy to tackle it. You may want to reevaluate: Is this genuinely important, or is it a 'should' or 'ought' that might be removed from your list?"*
- *"How well does the way you spend your time and money align with your heart?"*
- *"If you had total freedom to rearrange your life today to align with your values,*

with no outside obstacles or objections, what would be your top priorities?"

- *"So far the solutions I've heard seem to all involve reducing your down time. Keep in mind that reducing down time is a discipline that takes energy as well. How could you make this change without reducing your down time?"*

Client Exercise: Where to Change

Take the eight categories on the Life Wheel—Work, Money, Living Environment, Personal Growth, Health and Recreation, Community, Family, and God—and place them on the grid below. For example, if your marriage is going well and you don't need to invest more energy than you are now in that area, put it in the upper right box. If you are very stressed by your living environment, but can't change it now, put it in the lower right. If finances need work and it's time to do something about it, it goes in the lower left. Once the table is filled out, start your change strategies first on the lower left, then upper left.

	Invest New Energy	Keep the Same for Now
Going Well		
Going Poorly		

Boundaries

While balance helps us assign proper priorities and limits on our tasks, boundaries help us place appropriate limits on relationships.

- *"Where in life do you feel the need for more effective boundaries?"*
- *"What structures do you have in place to keep work from consuming all of life?"* [i.e. turning off cell phone at home, a carpool that leaves work at 5:00 pm, etc.]
- *"What is stopping you from saying, 'No?'"*
- *"Think it through: what specifically would you have to do or say to stand up for yourself and stop this from happening?"*
- *"What is it costing you to not stand up for your boundaries here?"*
- *"What do you gain from letting this happen? Or putting it another way, what do you fear you'd lose if you set this boundary that you still want to keep?"*
- *"What need or drive in you are people taking advantage of when they get you to say, 'Yes,' when you want to say, 'No?' What would it take to close that door?"*
- *"What would help you find the courage or energy you need to stand your ground?"*

Client Exercise: Role Playing Difficult Conversations

Often setting boundaries means standing up to a power person in your life. Sometimes role playing that conversation can be a great confidence-builder for the client. Take the part of the individual they must stand up to, and play out the conversation. Try out some of the objections this person might raise, and help your client figure out how to address them.

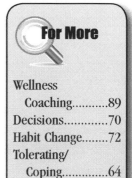

For More

SECTION V

Advanced Asking Skills

*"Millions saw the apple fall,
but Newton asked why."*

Bernard Baruch

In this section we'll explore some more advanced asking skills: from decision-making strategies and different types of affirmation to reframing techniques and ways to challenge the client. These skills tend to be much more specific to the particular coaching moment than the basic techniques covered earlier in this book. In other words, you'll rarely find yourself in a situation where you could use one of the example questions verbatim. Enough description and examples are provided for you to grasp the essence of each technique. With practice, you'll develop your own style of using these skills that will make the questions you ask your clients unique.

These skills also call for a more aggressive engagement with the client than some of the basics. That means the level of relationship you've established with the client is critical in using them well—they demand deeper intuitive insight, greater confidence, and more give and take between the client and coach. You may want to practice these more demanding skills with a peer coach before you try them out in a live situation.

So have fun taking your coaching to a higher level!

Affirmation

For some coaches, affirming others comes naturally. For others (like me!), it's a discipline. If you have to work at affirmation, these questions will help you discover new ways to offer affirmation with impact. There are three fundamental ways to affirm a person:

- **Celebrating Progress:** Affirming what the person **has done** or accomplished so far
- **Expressing Belief:** Sharing your confidence in what the coachee **will do** in the future
- **Naming Identity:** Positively articulating **who this person is** in their core being

These three methods are arranged in order of increasing impact. It is good to celebrate what you do (the externals); it is even better to have someone else believe in you and have confidence in your abilities; and it can be a life-changing experience to have the core of your being brought to light and affirmed by someone you trust and respect.

Celebrating Progress

Celebrating progress focuses on what the person has done.

- *"What has this person accomplished that should be celebrated?"*
- *"What specific progress has been made since we've been working together?"*
- *"What has s/he done that I can really say a hearty 'Yes!' to?"*
- *"How am I affirming the small steps forward that this person is taking? How could I do better?"*

Expressing Belief

Expressing belief is verbalizing what you believe this person is capable of doing.

- *"What do I want to affirm about this person's efforts or commitment?"*
- *"What do I believe about this person's future, based on what I've seen so far?"*
- *"What skills, habits and abilities does this person have that I see leading to future success?"*
- *"What is this person truly capable of in life? What potential is present here?"*
- *"What future do I see for this person that s/he may not have the confidence to see for him or herself? How can I believe in this person where s/he most needs to be believed in?"*

Naming Identity

Naming identity calls out the true inner self. It affirms your character and who you are.

- *"What character qualities do I admire in this person?"*
- *"What is the true value of this individual? What inner greatness and incredible potential have I seen in him/her?"*
- *"What can I name of this person's call or identity?"*
- *"At your best, who you are is _____."*
- *"What is the hidden treasure inside this person, that maybe others don't see?"*

Material taken from the *Peer Coach Training Workbook* by Tony Stoltzfus

---

Application

Questions to ask yourself to help you effectively affirm those you coach.

Exercise: Powerful Affirmation

Take one person you are coaching, and prepare to offer some powerful affirmation at your next appointment. Try to identify one thing in each of these three areas you can affirm. Tie your affirmation to actual events or things you've seen: specific affirmation connected to real life details is the most effective.

For More

Application

Asking tools for helping people look at decisions from multiple angles.

Decision Making

Developing the ability to make great decisions is a key part of living a purposeful life. Here are some questions for exploring the client's process for making decisions.

- *"How will you make that decision?"*
- *"What factors will make the most difference to you?"*
- *"What do you need to know to make a great decision?"*
- *"What would a great decision look like?"*
- *"How do you usually make decisions?"*
- *"What other decision strategies could you use? Which methods do you want to try?"*

Thirteen Decision-Making Strategies

Sometimes people are unaware of the decision-making process they are using, or of what other strategies are available. This list contains 13 common decision-making styles. Use it to help the client identify the strategies that are most comfortable and familiar, and what new strategies could be explored. Running a major decision through several strategies can be very revealing.

Exercise: Decision Making Strategies

Get together with a peer coach or friend who faces a major decision. First, explore how they've thought through things to this point. Can you help them identify their preferred decision-making strategy?

Then walk the person through at least three more of the strategies at right. What did you both learn by trying some new approaches and looking at the decision from different angles?

1. **Rational:** *"What are the pros and cons of pursuing each option? Which is most advantageous?"*
2. **Intuitive:** *"What is your gut saying? What feels right to you?"*
3. **Relational:** *"How will this course of action affect the people around you? Who will benefit, who will be hurt?"*
4. **Principled:** *"How do the key principles and priorities you live by apply here?"*
5. **Alignment:** *"How well does this decision align with your passions, your values, and your calling?"*
6. **Decisive:** *"What approach would most quickly lead you to a decision here?"*
7. **Adaptive:** *"What decisions could be left open to allow for new information or options? What things must be decided now that cannot be put off for later?"*
8. **Counsel:** *"What does your spouse think? How about some key friends or advisors?"*
9. **Team:** *"What do your team members think? What would happen if you decided as a team?"*
10. **Spiritual:** *"What decision would best align with your faith? What is God saying to you on this?"*
11. **Negative Drives:** *"What fears or inner drives are influencing your response? How could you remove those things from the equation so you can make a better decision?"*
12. **Cost:** *"What would it cost in terms of time and resources to do this? What would it cost you if you **don't** do this? What's the cost if you don't decide or let circumstances overtake you?"*
13. **Risk/Reward:** *"What is the payoff for each option? The risk? Can you live with the worst-case outcome? What steps could minimize the risk if you went with this?"*

Perspectives

One of the strengths of team decision-making is that you hear different perspectives on the problem from people with different personalities or positions. Decisions taken alone tend to see things from only one point of view. One very effective coaching technique is to walk the individual through several different viewpoints as they approach the decision:

- *You are a high 'I' on the DiSC inventory. What would a high 'D' do here? How about an 'S?'"*
- *"Take two people you know well, and talk me through how they would make this decision. What factors would be important to them? What would they prioritize? What can you learn from how they would approach this decision?"*
- *"Take a few minutes and walk me through the perspectives of the people this decision will affect. How does this change their lives? What is important to them here? How would they feel about each option?"*
- Create scenarios that illustrate the impact of the decision. For instance: *"Imagine you are a customer that's been doing business with your firm for many years. One day you get a notice that the policy we've been discussing is changing. What do you think of the change? How does it affect your business? Your future?"*
- *"Imagine you are at the end of your life looking back on this decision. From that perspective, what will seem most important? What will seem less important than it does now?"*
- *"You've invested a lot in this project so far. Step back for a minute and imagine that you had invested nothing up to this point—that it wouldn't cost you a dime or a minute of your time to walk away. How would that affect your decision?"*

Quotes...

"One does not discover new lands without consenting to lose sight of the shore."

Andre Gide

Taking on a New Commitment

Leaders are people who can see opportunities and want to pursue new things to make life richer. So when you coach leaders, you are almost always coaching busy people. That means that when new opportunities come along, the key challenge is keeping life in balance. These questions are focused around exploring whether to say "Yes!" to a new opportunity:

- *"What's exciting about this new opportunity? What makes this worth pursuing?"*
- *"What concerns do you have about this? What will it cost?"*
- *"How does this align with your purpose and mission in life?"*
- *"Take a look at this new commitment from a resource perspective. Sketch out a plan for where the time and energy will come from to do this well."*
- *"I get the impression your schedule is pretty full already—it is for most leaders. So what will you stop doing to make room for this new commitment?"*
- *"Do you feel any external pressure to go a certain way? What is your heart saying?"*
- *"Can this wait? What are the implications of putting the decision on hold for a bit?"*
- *"If you say 'Yes' now, how likely is it that in a month you'll wish you'd said, 'No?'"*

Being vs. Doing

Helping the client tune in to how s/he is being shaped by the decision itself and the process of making the decision can be a powerful conversation.

- *"Who are you **becoming** through this decision? How is it shaping your identity?"*
- *"What can you learn from this process about becoming a great decision-maker?"*
- *"What do your emotions in this decision reveal about the inner you? How do you want to respond to those insights?"*
- *"What does being faced with this decision now say about where you're at in life?"*

Application

Tools for increasing, finding or reconnecting with what motivates the client.

Motivation and Habit Change

Sometimes it is hard to find the motivation to choose what we know deep down we really want. And even after we've chosen, change is still a lot of work. Use these motivational techniques to help clients connect with their inner motivation, or find extra energy to tackle needed tasks that seem like a lot of work.

Reminders

The first step in changing a habit is becoming aware enough of the behavior that you catch yourself before you do it (if your goal is to stop smoking, you want to remember that objective before you light up, not after you realize the pack is empty). Setting up a remindering system can be an important part of making a change.

- *"How will you remember to do that each day?"*
- *"What kind of structure can you place around yourself to make sure you remember to do that consistently?"*
- *"What has worked for you in the past when you needed to be reminded to do something like this?"*
- *"How can you become more aware of when you drop into this negative thinking pattern? What clues can you pay attention to?"*
- *"What circumstances seem to set this pattern off? How could you become more aware of those triggers so you catch yourself before you go down this road?"*

The variety of reminders people find helpful is amazing. I've seen a post-it note on the steering wheel change someone's life. Other ideas: a live-strong bracelet, signs in the office or on the bathroom mirror, programming a daily reminder into your PDA, keeping a progress chart on the fridge, reviewing your goal in your quiet time each morning, an affirmation or a verse you repeat each day, a guided reflection on the day (Ignatius of Loyola's Examen is used by many), etc.

Regrets

Another version of the "Reconnecting with Your Motivation" technique in the sidebar is to experience what it would be like to **not** reach the goal. Help the person visualize a future where nothing changes, or the dream has not been pursued, or no action is taken. If the goal is truly important, the client may experience a deep sense of regret or loss as they think about not acting—and in that regret they may find the energy to move forward.

- *"You've been thinking about the cost of taking this step—that makes sense. But take a minute and look from the other side: what would it cost you if you **didn't** take this step?"*
- *"What if you chose not to act on this. What would life be like if nothing was different here in a year? How about in three years? How would that affect you?"*
- *"Let's say you are 80 years old, looking back on your life, and you never pursued this dream. Reflect on that for a minute or two. How does that feel to you?"*

Rewards

Reaching important goals usually requires doing some things we don't look forward to or don't like. Rewarding yourself for completing a step is a great way to increase motivation. It lets you focus on the reward at the end, instead of getting caught up in what a drudgery or sacrifice the

Hints & Tips

Reconnecting with Your Motivation

When a client seems to have lost energy for a goal, try taking them out of the present (where the costs and obstacles are) and into a future where that dream has actually come to pass. Use visual language to help the person enter that future and live in it: see it, taste it, celebrate it, revel in it. (See the Ideal Future Technique on page 42). Experiencing what it would be like to reach the goal for a few minutes can recharge the person and renew their motivation to work toward it.

step itself entails.

- *"What's something you could reward yourself with when you get this done?"*
- *"That sounds like hard work. How will you celebrate it when you reach your goal?"*
- *"What reward could you put at the end of this that would help you look forward to tackling this?"*
- *"Let's celebrate—that's a great accomplishment! How can you stand back (or share this moment with those you love) and say, 'That was very good!' this week?"*

Replacement

Sometimes trying not to do something just makes you focus on it all the more. A great strategy for removing a negative thinking pattern or an unhealthy behavior from your life is to fill the void with something better. For instance, want to watch less TV? What else could you replace it with that you really look forward to?

- *"It sounds like letting go of that will take some self-denial. That usually comes easier if you replace what you are giving up with something better you are moving toward. What do you want to replace this with?"*
- *"What does that behavior or thinking pattern give you that keeps you coming back to it? How could you meet that need in a more healthy way?"*
- *"If you're going to* **stop** *doing _____, what positive thing can you* **start** *doing to fill the void?"*

Accountability

Accountability is especially helpful with habit change. One way to deliver added value to your coachees is to help them get accustomed to being accountable to peers (instead of only to their coach). The best accountability partners are ones who are in the person's world (having them around is a reminder all by itself), who are for the coachee, who can be counted on to ask, and who have the courage to not just let the coachee off the hook.

- *"Would accountability to increase your chances of success?"*
- *"What qualities would you appreciate in an accountability partner?"*
- *"Who would be an effective accountability partner for this task?"*
- *"What do you need from this person?"*
- *"What will you ask this person to do for you?"*
- *"What accountability question would you like to be asked?"*

Exercise: Habit Change

Take a daily habit you'd like to change in your life and create a reward, a replacement strategy and some personal accountability for making the change. After a few weeks, stop and reflect: what impact did each tool have? Which worked best for you? Then find a client who wants to change a habit and help that person implement several of these strategies around their change goal.

Hints & Tips

Closed, specific, direct, accountability questions tend to work best. Vague questions such as, *"How is the diet going?"* produce answers like, "Pretty good," (which could mean anything). A better question is, *"How many days did you stick to your diet plan this week?"* or even *"Did you stick to your diet every day this week?"* There is no wiggle room there—the coachee must give an honest, specific accounting of what actually took place.

For More

Challenge

A key service coaches provide is challenging their clients. Challenge comes in many forms: pointing out inconsistencies, asking the person to reach higher, offering new perspectives, holding to boundaries and standards in the coaching relationship, or naming what you see in the person.

No matter what form it comes in, what makes the coaching approach to challenge unique is that it is forward-looking: instead of confronting (telling) you about how you screwed up in the past, coaches focus more on calling you to rise up and become your very best in the future.

I call that "Positive Challenge": pointing people forward to embrace all they were created to be, instead of looking back and pointing out where they have fallen short. Positive challenge also has the benefit of positioning you as a partner in reaching for a great future, whereas confrontation tends to position you as an adversary to the client. There are still times to be blunt and confront; but if you cultivate the techniques below, you'll find that you can often help a person see a blind spot or inconsistency with a much gentler approach.

Positive Challenge

Here are some examples of how to transform confrontation into positive challenge:

- **Telling Mode:** *"That decision isn't going to get you where you want to go."*
- **Better:** *"Take a minute and envision the future that you really want. Is this decision going to get you there, or is there a better way?"*

- **Telling Mode:** *"I don't think you are responding very well to the problem."*
- **Better:** *"If you were going to treat this conflict in a way you could look back on later in life with absolutely no regrets, what would you do?"*

- **Telling Mode:** *"This is all about you. You don't seem to care about anyone's interests but your own."*
- **Better:** *"I believe there is more in you than you've shown me so far. I want to see your absolute best—so that if I knew nothing else about you except how I saw you respond here, I'd believe you had the heart of a great leader. What will you do?"*

Asking for More

Sometimes coaches challenge goals and objectives as being too small:

- *"What if you set out to accomplish that goal in two years instead of five?"*
- *"Push yourself a bit. What if we increased the goal by 50%, or even doubled it?"*
- *"What would it look like for you to settle for less here? To give your very best?"*
- *"Will that goal stretch you and push you to grow? How would the goal have to expand for this to become a great growth experience as well as getting something important done?"*

The Open Question Challenge

Before you jump in and challenge a coachee, give the person the chance to challenge themselves. The beauty of this approach is that it doesn't use any relational capital, and you can always move on to try something else if it doesn't work.

- *"You mentioned you weren't totally committed to this venture. Say more about that."*
- *"Let's say you do decide to just quit. What are the implications of that decision?"*

- *"I heard you say that you were scared to pray about this. Unpack that for me."*
- *"So things aren't working out very well. What do you think needs to change?"*

Observations

An observation juxtaposes two or more statements the client has made that don't appear to add up. For instance, you might recall a client's stated value and then replay something the person has just said for comparison. The key to this technique is to make your observation without prejudice: recite the facts only, and then ask an open, neutral question that forces the person to grapple with their own statements.

- *"You mentioned earlier that your top priority right now is creating a more healthy lifestyle. Talk a bit about how that value fits with this new commitment you are contemplating at work."*
- *"I'm hearing words like 'maybe' and 'probably' and 'should' and 'ought' pretty often as you talk about this. What do you think is behind those words?"*
- *"Over the last month you've strongly voiced a need to meet regularly with your staff. Today I'm hearing you talk about cutting staff meetings entirely. Can you comment on that?"*
- *"We've been talking about your value for quantity and quality time with family. You also have a full-time job, you are taking 12 hours of graduate courses and you have a side business that keeps you busy every Saturday. Describe to me how your family values align with the schedule you are keeping."*

Ownership Questions

Ownership questions are often used in interpersonal conflicts, where we all have a tendency to get stuck in blaming the other individual. Ownership questions work in three ways: helping the person take responsibility for what has happened (past), helping them take ownership for solving the problem (future), and helping them tune into the situation as an opportunity for growth in character.

Taking Responsibility (responsibility for the past actions)

- *"What part did you play in creating this situation?"*
- *"What do you need to take responsibility for here?"*
- *"We've talked about the other person for a while: how about if we talk about you? What's your part in this?"*
- *"Since we can't change the other person anyway, let's focus on how you can learn and grow from this. What could you have done differently here?"*

Being Proactive (responsibility for the future actions)

- *"How would you like to move this forward?"*
- *"For the sake of argument, let's say that the other individual doesn't change—that if this is going to get better, it will be because you take the initiative. What would you do then?"*
- *"Does this person (or circumstance) really control your responses? Or do you have the power to rise up and make something great come out of this?"*

Transformational change commonly requires a trigger event: a significant experience or relational situation that provides the unusually strong motivation needed to fundamentally reevaluate our identity. What that means is that the time to challenge a strongly held belief, attitude or habit is *in the context of a teachable moment* that brings it to the surface. Without a trigger event, bringing up an issue you see out of the blue will not be very effective in producing lasting change.

Challenge (cont'd)

- *"You are a very capable individual. What if you took the bull by the horns and made everyone's life better by coming up with a permanent fix for this?"*
- *"Now that you've had a chance to get that off your chest, let's get down to business. What can you do to turn this around and make something good out of it?"*

Growing in Character (responsibility for inward growth)

- *"Conflict and difficulty always contain the opportunity to grow in character. Where's the opportunity for you to grow in this situation?"*
- *"What do your responses here reveal about who you are? What do you want to do with that?"*
- *"How could you leverage your frustration in this situation as motivation to grow into more of the person you've always wanted to be?"*
- *"What would it be worth to you if you could learn something from this situation that would keep it from ever happening again? Would you like to go there?"*

Coaching Exercise: Ownership Questions

Think of a real-life conflict you are involved in, or of something that a friend or co-worker does that bugs you that you haven't yet addressed. Have your peer think of a situation as well. Then take turns coaching each other through your conflicts. Try to ask an ownership question from each of the three categories above during the conversation.

Then debrief afterward. How did your partner do at asking ownership questions? What was genuinely helpful? What kind of context must you create in the coaching conversation to ask ownership questions effectively?

Naming the Issue vs. Confrontation

I define confrontation as "naming the issue, defining your actions as wrong, and challenging you to change your behavior in that area." The aspect of confrontation that most easily becomes adversarial is the "defining your actions as wrong" part.

Often a better option is to name the core issue, but without adding that you think the person is wrong and needs to change. The key to doing this well is to do it without prejudice. Simply say what you think is going on, without shame or blame or accusation. Then let the coachee figure out what it means and what response is called for. Naming the issue is like confrontation, but without the slap on the wrist.

Here are two examples of the difference between confrontation and naming the issue. Which would you respond best to?

- **Confrontation:** *"That was wrong. You should have checked in with your spouse before you made that decision."*
- **Naming the Issue:** *"One thing that is affecting the outcome here is that the*

decision was made without consulting your spouse beforehand."

- **Confrontation:** *"Your boss is mad at you because you overstepped your authority and took the situation into your own hands. You need to deal with this pattern of usurping authority in your life."*

- **Naming the Issue:** *"Think back for a minute: this is the third situation we've talked through where you've gotten in trouble with someone over you—and each one involved a different authority figure who felt you went too far. The common denominator in these situations is you: what do you think you might be doing that is consistently producing this outcome?"*

Naming the Issue Examples

Here are some actual questions and statements from live coaching situations where I've named the issue for a client:

- *"That statement doesn't sound consistent with your values."*
- *"Can I be honest with you? Your response sounds a little whiny. How could you refocus on getting the outcome you want instead of on how you're being treated?"*
- *"I'm hearing the old voices of fear and hesitancy as you talk. What would the real John Smith say here?"*
- *"I haven't heard anything yet about how this decision will affect the people around you or what their opinions are. What does your wife think of this? Your kids?"*
- *"What I'm hearing so far is that you are going to decide by getting other people's advice and following it. But what is **your** heart saying? What would it take for you to have the confidence to make a great decision without depending on others?"*
- *"You have a tendency to wander sometimes—can I have your permission to interrupt to help us stay on track if we are going down a bunny trail?"*
- *"I've noticed that you have a hard time pinning yourself down to action steps at the end of the coaching conversation. I was fairly aggressive this time in getting you to make a decision—is that what you want from me as a coach, or not?"*
- *"It seems that you are allowing this person's actions to determine your responses. You have given this person a lot of power over you—is that what you really want?"*

Coaching Exercise: Challenge

Think of a real situation in the past where one of your own issues or blind spots created a problem or a conflict. Role play it with your peer partner coaching you. Try to recapture how you thought and felt while you were still functioning out of your blind spot. The coach should walk you through the situation, find something in your responses that could be challenged, and try out several different challenge techniques on you. Then switch places and redo the exercise. What did you learn about challenge? What techniques seem to work better or worse on you? Why?

For More

Reframing/Perspective Change

A key reason people seek to work with a coach is to get perspective on their lives. So when we ask for perspective, or say we've lost perspective, what do we mean? Here are four types of perspective we look for:

1. **Proportion**
   The big picture. Seeing the real importance and true interrelationship of things.

2. **Objectivity**
   Rational Thinking. Detaching myself emotionally to see things as they really are.

3. **Viewpoint**
   Comprehensive thinking. Looking at the situation from a variety of different angles.

4. **Clarity**
   Knowing that you know, and having the assurance to act confidently.

There are many ways coaches can reframe the conversation to change perspective. Below are several sample sets of questions that increase Objectivity and Proportion or alter the Viewpoint.

The Perspective of Balance

- *"What's going on in other areas of life that is putting pressure on this area or making it more difficult for you to reach your goal?"*
- *"Think about the importance of this relative to your relationships, family, spiritual life, health, etc. How important is this in the grand scheme of things?"*
- *"What do you have to be thankful for in your life right now? What's going well?"*

The Perspective of Time

- *"What will this decision look like in ten years? What will seem most crucial then?"*
- *"Imagine you are 75 years old, looking back on your life. What would you most regret if you took this road? What would you be most proud of?"*
- *"If you were still doing this in five years, how would it affect you? Your family? Your destiny?"*

The Perspective of Passion/Purpose

- *"Let's say this situation is custom-designed to prepare you for what you are born to do. How would that change your perspective on your circumstances?"*
- *"Let's say your boss or your team came to you and said, 'We want you to pursue the thing that most makes your heart leap.' What would you do then?"*
- *"What is the compelling reason to make this move? Why must this be done?"*
- *"What is the opportunity here? How can this move you toward your destiny?"*

The Viewpoint of Others

- *"How is this affecting your family, relationships, friends and others around you?"*
- *"Just as an exercise, let's try on the perspectives of the other players. How would this look through your boss's eyes? To your team? Your customers? The media?"*
- *"OK—I've heard you make the argument for this change. Let me hear you make the*

It's not easy to leave your own viewpoint and take on another. Creating a scenario or vision-picture of what things look like from another point of view can help. For instance, create a future perspective by drawing a picture of the client sharing a victory with his or her grand kids, or experiencing the joy of accomplishment when the project is over. Or help the person walk a mile in a boss, spouse or co-worker's shoes in order to see with new eyes. If you sketch out some initial details, often the person will be able to enter in, complete the picture, and gain a new perspective.

case against *it. If you were going to convince me that we shouldn't do this, what would you say?"*

The Perspective of Freedom

- *"For the sake of argument, let's assume that you have the power to change this situation—that you can take action and make a difference. What would you do if you saw yourself as being in control instead of controlled?"*
- *"What about this situation is under your control, and what isn't? What can you do about the part that you can change? What about the part you can't?"*
- *"I see you as a person of great initiative and ability—what if you saw yourself that way here?"*

The Perspective of Motives

- *"What is motivating you to go in this direction?"*
- *"What are you proactively reaching toward? What are you trying to get away from?"*
- *"Let's take a hypothetical look at some different possible motivations here. If you were going to act solely to make life better now, what would that look like? How about if your overwhelming concern was the future? Or the organization's future? Or your relationships with people?"*
- *"What do you want to admit to yourself about how you are making this choice?"*

The Perspective of Confidence

- *"Which alternative provides a healthy amount of stretching—not overwhelming, not boring, but challenging you to step out and use your full capabilities?"*
- *"If you had unlimited resources and couldn't fail, how would it change your perspective?"*
- *"Imagine yourself with total confidence that you could make this happen—you just knew that you knew. How would that change your approach?"*

Clarity

This type of question can help clients come to a place of clarity and confidence that they have adequate perspective to move forward:

- *"What would it look like to know the answer to this question? How might that knowing come about?"*
- *"How will you know that you know?"*
- *"When you've been in situations like this in the past that turned out well, how did you feel in the midst of it? Did you go through it with total confidence and certainty, or did you have doubts along the way?"*
- *"What do you still need to feel confident that this course of action is the right one?"*
- *"OK—let's run with that. What's the worst that could happen if you pursue this? Can you live with that outcome?"*
- *"Revisit the underlying rationale: what's the compelling reason for doing this?"*

Some material taken from CD *Powerful Questions: Changing Perspective* by Tony Stoltzfus

---

Hints & Tips

Personality types are another useful perspective tool. If the client knows a particular personality system, ask him/her to tell you what this situation would look like from the perspective of some of the other types (especially if one of those other types is on the team). Or as the coach you can ask yourself that question to come up with new viewpoints and new insights on the situation.

For More

Reflection

When coaching leaders, you are often working with people who are very accomplished doers, but less adept at being and reflecting. Coaches can help active leaders develop the discipline of reflection to help them maximize learning from what they do in life.

Reflective Styles

One area that often needs addressing is identifying a reflective style that works for the client.

- *"What kind of time and place are most conducive to reflection for you?"*
- *"Do you reflect best by talking through things out loud* [extrovert style] *or by pondering or writing by yourself* [introvert style]*?"*
- *"Share one of your best experiences with reflection. What kind of setting were you in, what did you do to reflect, and what did you learn?"*
- *"How have you intentionally built reflection or 'thought time' into your life?"*
- *"Journaling can mean writing complete sentences or bullet lists, being orderly or doodling in the margins, dictating, typing or writing longhand. What kind of journaling style best helps you order your thoughts?"*
- *"Have you journaled in the past? What worked for you?"*

Reflection Questions

Reflection questions ask us to stop and examine what is happening at a deeper level.

- *"What is behind that?"*
- *"What would it take for you to get to the bottom of that?"*
- *"If you could get the answer to one question, what would that question be?"*
- *"What is driving your responses? What internal pressures are you responding to?"*
- *"What do you want?"*
- *"What's the right thing to do?"*
- *"What factors influence this decision?"*
- *"Where are you going? Where will this lead you?"*
- *"You mentioned that this first started bugging you last year. What changed?"*
- *"What do you need to tune into? What is going on under the surface?"*
- *"What does your heart say?"*
- *"When you look at this from a faith perspective, what do you see?"*
- *"What emotions are you experiencing in this situation?"*
- *"What do you expect here? How are unspoken expectations influencing this situation?"*

Solidifying the Learning

Any time a coachee makes a major breakthrough, you can get extra mileage out of the event by reflecting about how it happened. Important insights about change and how to succeed in other areas of life can come by tuning into what makes change work in *this* area. A second important reflection task is to make the change or insight stick. Helping the client reflect on how to make the change permanent can make a big difference in your overall coaching effectiveness

- *"How did this change happen? What events and circumstances led to the breakthrough?"*

- *"What can you learn from this experience about making successful changes elsewhere in life?"*
- *"What universal principles of growth or change can you distill from this experience that can be passed on to others?"*
- *"How can we make this change stick, so you never have to relearn this again?"*
- *"What structures could you build into your life to help ensure that this change is permanent?"*

Following the Emotion

All emotions contain information. We feel things for a reason. And emotions can tell us things that reason can't, because emotions bypass many of our conscious defenses and provide a window into our heart. Following the emotion is the technique of tuning into the emotional cues you see, reflecting them back to the client, and asking the person to explore them further.

- *"What are your emotions saying?"*
- *"Anger is a response to perceived loss or injustice—what's behind that feeling of anger?"*
- *"What is your body saying? Close your eyes for a few moments and really pay attention. What sensations do you have? What do they mean?"*
- *"You sound frustrated—what is frustrating you? What beliefs or expectations feed into that sense of frustration?"*
- *"You seem really cheerful and energized this morning—what's going on there?"*
- *"Here's another way to get in touch with how well your role fits you. Close your eyes and visualize yourself at work—at your desk, going through the daily tasks. What feelings or sensations do you have as you visualize yourself there?"*
- *"I'm hearing some hesitancy in your voice about taking that action. Can you unpack that?"*

Quotes...

"A life unexamined is not worth living."

Socrates

Client Exercise: Learning from a Significant Experience

Often we go through important experiences (especially the difficult ones) and learn only a fraction of what we could from the situation. These questions help a client glean the most from a significant experience in their life, past or present.

- *"**WHAT** happened? Describe the main events that made up this experience."*
- *"**WHEN** did you first become aware that something significant was going on? Were there clues that something important was happening that you missed? What would help you become aware earlier in the process next time?"*
- *"**HOW** did your actions influence the outcome of this? What actions do you want to celebrate, and what would you like to change next time around?"*
- *"**WHY** did this touch you deeply? What changes in attitudes or beliefs does this experience push you to consider?"*

For More

Feedback and Evaluation

Self-Evaluation for Coachees

Application

Questions for evaluating your own coaching as well as the client's progress.

At times it can be very helpful to have the coachee evaluate their own performance in a task or role. I also like to periodically have them self-evaluate their progress toward the coaching goal. People often forget to stop and celebrate progress along the way.

- *"What did you do well? What would you do differently if you could do this again?"*
- *"What progress can we celebrate here? What do we still need to work on?"*
- *"How would you evaluate your progress?"*
- *"On a scale of one to ten, evaluate your progress toward your goal. What step would raise that number to the next notch?"*

Feedback for Coaches

Coaching Exercise: Self-Evaluation

Take a coaching session you did in the last week or two and self-evaluate it using at least four of the questions at right. Create at least one action step for improving your coaching from what you learn.

It's also a good practice to get some periodic feedback from your clients. If you want feedback, you'll generally have to ask for it. The principle is, "Unless you establish a healthy process for getting feedback, all the feedback you get will be unhealthy."

- *"On a scale of one to ten, how helpful was this session for you? What would have made it better?"*
- *"I try to adjust my coaching style to get the best fit with the needs of my clients. Are there any adjustments we need to make here?"*
- *"Are we working on what's most important to you?"*
- *"Is there anything you'd like to talk about or do more of that isn't on our agenda?"*
- *"What's your emotional state when you leave our sessions? Are you energized, overwhelmed, hopeful, discouraged, or what?"*

Self-Evaluation for Coaches

Taking time after your sessions for a few minutes of self-evaluation can be a great learning experience. Here are some questions you might ask yourself:

- *"What did I do well in this session? What would I do differently next time?"*
- *"What is this person's personality type? How am I coaching in a way that works for their type as opposed to just using my natural personality style?"*
- *"Are we making good progress toward the coaching objectives? What adjustments would lead to greater progress?"*
- *"What intuitive cues did I see today that I need to remember for the future?"*
- *"What is going on under the surface with this person? How could we tap into that more deeply?"*
- *"Where is my challenge/affirmation balance at with this client? Which of those two things do I need to do more of?"*
- *"What movement do I see that I need to affirm or give feedback on the next time we meet?"*
- *"What do I need to challenge? Where could I effectively ask for more?"*
- *"Is this person being energized by our sessions? How could I increase the amount of positive motivation that comes out of our times together?"*

For More

Coaching Niches

"Coaching will become the model for leaders in the future… I am certain that leadership can be learned, and that terrific coaches… facilitate learning."

Warren Bennis

In this section, I've joined with a dozen other professional coaches to introduce you to some of the specialized coaches niches that are out there. It's like ordering a "sampler" of appetizers at a restaurant: you get a little taste of everything. If you are new to coaching, you might look these over and find one that really appeals to you. Even if you are an experienced coach with a well-defined niche of your own, clients who come to you for one thing will often open other areas like these to you as well. Sooner or later that relationship coaching client will start talking about his small business, or your life coaching client will have a marriage issue to deal with, or the person who came to you for career coaching will want to work on diet and exercise. In other words, at one time or another you may coach a little in almost all of these areas.

What's Here

For each niche, we've included a page or two with a short description of that specialty, some of its unique challenges, and a tool or list of common questions a coach might use in that area. The names and web addresses of the coaches who contributed are at in the sidebar of each page.

Obviously, a page or two about each specialty is not a comprehensive treatment, and this section only covers some of the more common coaching niches. But this will give you a flavor for what's out there, plus a tool or two for those times when you might venture into a less familiar area.

SECTION VI

Small Business Coaching

By Bill Zipp

Employee problems, debt loads, production deadlines, and equipment breakdowns impact all businesses. But unlike other professions, a small business owner often faces these challenges with family members as key employees, major investors—or both! In small business coaching, business and personal issues are intertwined. Coaching the business works toward a strong, self-sustaining company, while personal coaching builds healthy relationships and a balanced lifestyle.

A frequent coaching area on the business side is marketing. For many business owners, marketing is a dirty word. However, the fact that marketing has been misused doesn't mean we can ignore it. There is a marketing method that is honest, true to our values, and honoring to our prospects and customers. In fact, for genuine, long-term business growth, this is the **only** way to do marketing. I call this *Meaningful Marketing*. It's an approach to advertising based on truthful, strategic content crafted in an honest, compelling way. Here are nine coaching questions for designing meaningful marketing initiatives:

1. *"Who is your **target customer?** That is, who is the person that is the best fit for using your company's products and services?"*
2. *"Describe your target customers: how old are they? Where do they live? Where do they work? What are their families like? What are their hopes? Their dreams? Their fears? Write out everything you know about your target customer."*
3. *"What are three to five problems that your products or services solve for your target customer?"*
4. *"From the list above, what is the **biggest problem** your products or services solve for your target customer?"*
5. *"What are three to five unique advantages of using your company's products or services?"*
6. *"From the list above, what is the **greatest advantage** of using your products or services?"*
7. *"What are all the ways a prospect or customer can contact you? (Visiting your store, calling you on the phone, going to your web site, etc.)"*
8. *"From the list above, what makes the most strategic sense as a person's **first point of contact** with your business?"*

Coaching Exercise: Create Your Marketing Message

As a coach, you are a small business owner, too! Work through the steps of this exercise for your own coaching practice.

Authors

Bill Zipp (www. BillZipp.com) is President of Leadership Link, co-author of *The Business Coaching Toolkit*, and seasoned small business specialist who has worked with hundreds of business leaders.

Exercise: Designing a Meaningful Marketing Message

Most marketing errs in trying to be all things to all people. Meaningful Marketing does just the opposite. Take your answers to questions four, six, and eight above and write a 75-word, 30-second commercial for your target customer. Keep at this project until every word packs a punch—it will really pay off!

9. *"Where are all the places you can use this marketing message? Remember to 'stay on message' in every one of these venues!"*

Organizational Coaching

By Jane Creswell

Organizational Coaching is the systematic coaching of individuals within an organization to support organizational change. The key difference from normal business or executive coaching is that the organization itself has a culture (like an individual client's personality type). To effectively work at changing a corporate culture, the coach needs to understand that culture—it's strengths, weaknesses, and untapped potential—and take that knowledge into account as s/he coaches the individuals within the culture. A unique challenge of organizational coaching is working on both the individual and corporate levels at the same time.

Coachability

A major success factor is determining whether the organization is coachable. One way to examine the organization's readiness to change is to look at the culture's history:

- *"Has this company been an early adopter of industry trends, or has it been dragged kicking and screaming into the future?"*
- *"Is this a risk-taking or risk-averse culture?"*
- *"Are current circumstances or business difficulties providing broad-based motivation for change within the organization?"*

Another important factor is getting coaching understood and embraced within the corporate culture. A typical strategy is to start with the most motivated and coachable individuals, and allow them to influence others in the organization on the value of the coaching process. Below are questions for coaching individuals with the organization:

- *"How does your life calling fit with the purpose of this organization?"*
- *"What do you want to accomplish here for yourself and for the sake of the organization?"*
- *"What drives you? What are you passionate about?"* [The coach is seeking to determine how well the individual's passions align with those of the organization.]

Questions for Leaders

These questions are directed toward the leader who is launching the coaching initiative:

- *"What is your purpose in wanting to create a coaching culture in this organization?"*
- *"What is the commitment level within this organization to creating a coaching culture?"*
- *"Do you have a budget for introducing coaching here? What is your time frame for creating a coaching culture?"*
- *"Is this a good time for your organization to invest in new processes and projects?"*
- *"What are your thoughts about including the rest of your leadership in this initiative? How would you get them on board? Who would you start with?"*
- *"Where could we start with a pilot project? What criteria would you use in designing that pilot?"*

Application

Hints on coaching whole teams or companies as opposed to just individuals.

Authors

Jane Creswell, MCC, (www. Internal-Impact. com) is passionate about inspiring and equipping organizations to establish systems for internal coaching.

Career Coaching

By Keith Webb

Career coaching focuses on aligning a client's passions, skills and values with their work. In a lifetime, we typically change careers ten times, and 90% of American workers don't like their jobs. Often this is because our jobs don't tap into our core passions and strengths. Career coaching offers clients the opportunity to discover their calling, strengths, values and desired contribution, then helps them align work or manage retirement for a more fulfilling life.

Changing Organizations

Job changes often stem from wanting to escape current challenging circumstances. Coaching with the questions below can decrease the chance that a client will jump from one unsatisfactory position to another. The questions on corporate culture are particularly useful for exploring non-profit, ministry or community-help positions.

1. Know Yourself
- *"What are you passionate about?"*
- *"What are your strengths, gifts, and key abilities?"*
- *"What do you want to learn, and how do you want to contribute?"*

2. Know the Corporate Culture
- *"How much do you believe in their mission?"*
- *"What are their real values?"*
- *"Who would you work with?"*

3. Know the Needs
- *"How much does the organization need me?"*
- *"How much do I need the organization?"*

Refocusing Vision

A common work-related problem is that even in best-fit careers, vision and passion tend to fade over time in the face of everyday workplace demands. Here are some questions for exploring, discovering and reigniting passion in the workplace.

- *"What was your original vision when you came here? How has it changed?"*
- *"What parts of your current job tasks (or role) are directly related to your vision?"*
- *"How could you increase the vision-related tasks, and decrease the others?"*

- *"What would you like to be doing five years from now?"*
- *"What part of that could you begin doing now?"*
- *"How do you need to plan and prepare so you can be in that role in five years?"*

- *"What would you say are your best strengths?"*
- *"What percentage of the time are you operating out of your strengths?"*
- *"How could you increase that, or creatively apply your strengths to today's challenges?"*

Authors

Keith Webb
(CreativeResults Management.com) is a coach and coach trainer who helps non-profit organizations, teams and individuals to multiply their cross-cultural impact.

Organizing Coach/Professional Organizer

By Rhonda Ruckel

Organizing coaches help professionals get their things in order, at home and at work. Where disorder robs energy and productivity, these coaches specialize in bringing order out of the chaos in everything from filing systems and document flow to organizing closets and bills.

Initial Assessment

- *"Describe for me what being organized looks like to you."*
- *"What is motivating you to get organized? What makes you want to start now?"*
- *"What is it costing you to be disorganized?"*
- *"Talk about an area where you are/were well organized. How did it get that way?"*
- *"What's your number one obstacle to getting organized?"*
- *"Who in your life would be willing to help, and whom would you allow to help?"*
- *"If you were going to start eating the elephant* [How do you eat an elephant? One bite at a time.] *what part would you get rid of or get under control first, and why?"*

Setting Priorities

- *"What is the compelling reason for doing _____?"*
- *"What is the payoff of this activity compared to the time you will invest in it?"*
- *"Is this event or activity time critical or day specific?"*
- *"Can this task be delegated? Who could do this at least 80% as well as you?"*
- *"What is the worst that could happen if this doesn't get done?"*

Sorting Tool

As you take clients through their piles or the miscellany mountains that clog their lives, a first step is to sort things into the following four categories. The categories are arranged in pairs: I have things I love or am ambivalent about; and things I need, or can let go of.

Category 1: *"Do you **Love** this?"*

Category 2: *"Are you **Ambivalent** about this or unsure of what to do with it?"*

- *"When did you last use/wear/reference this item?"*
- *"Who might make better use of this than you?"*
- *"Describe what you will lose if you let this go."*
- *"Would you spend money to replace this if you no longer have it? How much?"*
- *"Is it worth the space to store it?"*

Category 3: *"Can you **Let Go** of this?"*

- *"Do you want to give it away, sell it, pitch it, or what?"*

Category 4: *"Do you **Need** this?"*

- *"Do you have to be the one to store it?"*
- *"Can it be stored more efficiently? Do you need a better retrieval system?"*

These questions help determine what to do with each item. The final step is to take all the **Ambivalent** items and re-sort them into the **Love**, **Need**, or **Let Go** categories.

Application

Tools for clients who need to bring order to priorities and living environment.

Coaching Exercise: Sorting Tool

A good way to get familiar with the sorting tool at left is to try it on yourself. Find a room, closet, a file cabinet or other place you want to organize. Put the items into these four categories, then take the "Ambivalent" items and resort them into the other three categories. What did you learn in the process?

Authors

Rhonda Ruckel (www.MakeaChange Coaching.com) is a coach trainer and Professional Organizer specializing in coaching workflow and time management.

Application

Tips for coaching budding authors, including crafting an overall book concept.

Coaching Writers (Book Coaching)

By Jerome Daley

There are an amazing number of people who have a book inside them... but who need some help packaging their brilliance into something publishable. For coaches who are also published authors, there is a strong market for a combination of coaching and mentoring to help your client put feet to their writing dreams.

Overview of the Niche

Coaching writers frequently involves working in the following areas:

1. Educating them on publishing options (e-books, self-publishing, print-on-demand, book packagers, full-service houses, etc.).
2. Describing the points of access for large publishing houses, notably writers conferences and literary agents.
3. Tapping into their vision and making sure it is cohesive, compelling, and communicable.
4. Helping them craft their vision into a book proposal.
5. Editing their content at some level.
6. Helping them develop and stick to the discipline of actually writing something.

This type of coaching involves a lot more mentoring, advice-giving and consulting than typical coaching does, yet your expertise finds its greatest value in the context of active listening, powerful questioning, and the other foundational coaching methodologies.

The Book Concept

Below are ten questions that help a writer define the underlying concept for their book:

- *"What is the one thing you most want to say to your readers?"*
- *"Who do you want to say it to? Who is your target audience?"*
- *"What is the felt need that your message addresses?"*
- *"What is the impact your message will have on the reader?"*
- *"What will you say that has not been said before?"*
- *"What life experience will you draw from in communicating your message?"*
- *"How would you summarize your message in 50 words? In 100 words?"*
- *"How will you hook your reader's rapt attention in the first paragraph... and keep them hooked throughout the book?"*
- *"What are your natural spheres of influence for selling books? Who else?"*
- *"How involved do you want to be in marketing your book? How will this impact your lifestyle?"*

Bonus question: *"If you are actually able to achieve this dream of publishing your book, what will that get you?"*

Authors

Jerome Daley (www. PurposeCoach. net) is a leadership coach, author of five books, and managing editor of the *Journal of Christian Coaching*.

Wellness Coaching

By Sharon Graham, RN

Wellness coaching is helping people to create healthy lifestyles and "care for the only body they will ever have." As a holistic wellness and nutritional coach, I partner with clients to identify and overcome barriers to living a great life—not only in their physical body, but in their emotional and spiritual sides as well. Having a physical body that "works well" is vital to having stable, healthy emotions. And when one "feels" well physically and emotionally, spiritual life is also enhanced.

In order for each of us to live out our life purpose, we must have a body that isn't racked with pain and inflammation and a brain that is clear and focused. Concentrating on wellness and nutrition offers that to a client. As the client begins to get a glimpse of how their body can either work for them or against them, they get excited about moving forward with the coaching process.

General Wellness Assessment

- *"Describe how satisfied you are with your overall health and sense of well being."*
- *"If you continue in this present state of health, what will your health look like and how will you feel five years down the road? How about in ten years?"*
- *"What is motivating you to make nutritional and dietary changes now?"*
- *"How many servings of vegetables do you eat in a week? (French fries don't count.)"*
- *"What kind of margin do you have on a daily basis? Where's your stress level at?"*
- *"What is a realistic and comfortable clothing (or pant) size for you? How long has it been since you've worn that size? How realistic is your desired size?"*
- *"What would your life look like right now if you were truly healthy?"*

Wellness Wheel Assessment

Ask coachees to report their satisfaction with each of the eight areas on the diagram (you may need to explain them a bit first).

- *"On a scale of one to ten, how satisfied are you in each of these areas?"*
- *"Tell me what's behind that number. How did you arrive at that?"*
- *"If you could change one area tomorrow, which would it be? Why?"*
- *"In what area would a change give you the most results with the least effort?"*

Wellness Assessment

Water, Sleep, Immunity, Energy, Stress, Digestion, Weight, Exercise

Making Changes

- *"How committed are you to this step of walking 45 minutes per day, five days a week? What obstacles could get in your way?"*
- *"What will it take for you to STOP drinking soda?"*
- *"What has to happen for you to get to bed by 10:00 PM? What time do you need to begin winding down and preparing for bed?"*
- *"What type of exercise appeals to you? How could you consistently move more?"*

Relationship Coaching

By Dave McIllrath, MA

While relationship coaching covers the whole gamut of issues from dating to marriage, I focus on working with coachable couples and individuals who have experienced brokenness or betrayal in a relationship. This puts a premium on safety and ownership. Meeting people where they are at without judgment creates a wonderful context for change.

The *Facts/Thoughts/Feelings* tool below helps couples improve communication (or individuals reflect on a conflict) by separating out the facts of what actually happened from how they interpreted or felt about those facts. Walk the client or couple through these steps:

1. Facts

Facts are what both people would agree happened... without assumptions regarding intent. They are typically neutral: "When you left the house this morning, you didn't say goodbye."

- *"What are the facts of this situation? What actually happened?"*
- *"Can you describe what exact words were said or actions took place, without interpretation?"*

2. Thoughts

Ask the clients to express how they interpreted what happened. Thoughts are what they created in their own minds about it: "It seemed like you weren't paying attention to me at all."

- *"What did you make up about that?"* [I use this question intentionally, because it helps people embrace humility instead of taking on a, 'you made me feel...' posture.]
- *"How did you interpret those words or actions? What meaning did you give them?"*

3. Feelings

Ask the client to express the core feeling that's connected to their thoughts in a single word. Help clients own their emotions, as opposed to expressing them as something the other person did to them.

- *"Name the feeling you have about this in a word—like anger, sadness, joy, fear, shame, etc."*
- *"It seems like you've expressed that feeling as something your partner did to you. Can you express it as something you fully own as yours?"*

4. Future

The client makes a request of the other party to improve future communication. At first clients can misuse it ("In the future, can I ask that you not be such a jerk?"). This step becomes effective when clients begin to catch on that they can change the thoughts and feelings they associate with the facts. Ask the clients to make requests of each other in this format:

- *"In the future, this would work better for me if we _____."*
- *"One way you could help me understand you better in the future would be to ___."*

Authors

Dave McIllrath is President of TruthCoaching.com. He coaches those who have experienced brokenness to use past pain as a springboard for a thriving future.

Coaching Ministry Leaders

With contributions from Jerry Graham, John Purcell and Tony Stoltzfus

Ministry leaders have a uniquely challenging occupation. Leading a volunteer organization with high demands for leadership ability, relational skills, and personal morality and integrity means that just about every area of the leader's life gets involved in the coaching process. Calling, personal and spiritual disciplines, career transitions, and managing change are frequent coaching areas. Discouragement, burnout and reevaluation of call are also common issues. The questions below are targeted at pastors.

Application

Questions for working with the unique needs of pastors.

Caring for Pastors

Pastors tend to lack deep friendships and support networks outside their local congregations, which can limit their options for processing significant life and calling issues. The coaching relationship often becomes a primary vehicle for perspective, relational support and self-care.

- *"What kind of season of life are you in right now?"*
- *"What is God's name for you?"* or *"Who does God say that you are?"*
- *"How have you built rest and refreshment into your life? What is your Sabbath pattern?"*
- *"What if the impact of your ministry was that people actually copied the way you live? If you multiplied your lifestyle—your family life, work hours, stress level, exercise patterns, your enjoyment of life—into your congregation, how would you feel about that?"*
- *"What will it mean for you if your church continues basically as is for the next few years?"*

Coaching Pastors as Visionaries

Leading an organization of volunteers puts a premium on vision-casting skills. These questions touch on that area:

- *"What does God uniquely want to accomplish in your church? How about through your church?"*
- *"What is your church's plan and process for producing mature and equipped believers?"*
- *"If you died tonight, what effect would that have on your church? What does that say about you as a leader? About your leadership development efforts?"*
- *"If your church closed its doors tomorrow, what effect would that have on your community?"*
- *"How do you evaluate your effectiveness in accomplishing your mission? How do you know when you are on track?"*
- *"If I donated a million dollars to your ministry, what would you do with it?"*
- *"Describe for me, in vivid detail, what your church would look like if it were meeting all your expectations and dreams."*
- *"What do you believe has been holding you back from achieving these dreams (or at least making significant progress toward them)?"*

Authors

Jerry Graham (TheCoachingPair.com) has mentor-coached hundreds of trainees in addition to coaching many pastors and ministry leaders.

John Purcell (Transform-Coach.com) is a coach and consultant to churches that want to build more effective small group and discipleship ministries and develop "discipling leaders."

Application

Questions for small group coaches that touch on pastoral care and leadership issues.

Small Group Coaching

Contributions from Randall Neighbour and John Purcell

Small group coaching is typically done by a volunteer coach with a maximum of five group leaders as coachees. The small group system has clear objectives for what these leaders need to accomplish (around fostering members' spiritual growth), so much of the coaching agenda is derived from that mandate. Because these volunteer coaches have less training and experience, the coaching process tends to be more structured. Most churches select coaches who have been successful group leaders, and expect them to mentor as well as coach.

The Leader's Task

- *"What do you see God doing in the lives of the men or women in your group?"*
- *"What small growth steps are you seeing in your group members?"* [Too often, leaders only see big leaps in growth, and it doesn't usually happen that way.]
- *"How are you investing in your men's/women's lives outside the meeting times?"*
- *"How are the people in your group building relationships with each other? How do you see authenticity increasing in the group?"*
- *"How are you delegating tasks/responsibilities to your members to help them grow?"*
- *"How are you developing these men and women into their full potential as leaders?"*
- *"If I were watching your group, what group dynamics would I see?"*
- *"How are you engaging your core team in the planning/decision-making process?"*
- *"Complete this sentence for me about one of your group members: '_____ would be a great small group leader if...'"*

The Leader's Personal Life

Because a good small group coach cares about the person, not just the role the person fills, these questions drill down into their personal lives. Knowing your leaders deeply provides specific ways to encourage and pray for them.

- *"Talk to me about how you're balancing your relationships, work, family, and ministry. How do things now compare to three months ago? What's caused the change, if any?"*
- *"What is God saying to you these days?"* [If the leader has no devotional life, s/he will have little to share when asked this question.]
- *"What did you take away from the last book you read?"*
- *"How can I specifically pray for you?"*
- *"On a scale of one to ten, how would your spouse rate the health and intimacy of your marriage?"*
- *"What is your greatest personal challenge as it pertains to leading your group?"*
- *"What does God have for you next in ministry? What concrete steps are you taking to move toward that?"*

Randall Neighbour (TouchUSA.org and SmallGroupFriends.com) is a well known speaker and author, whose ministry supports churches with resources, consulting and on-site training.

John Purcell (www.Transform-Coach.com) is a coach and consultant to churches that want to build more effective small group and discipleship ministries and develop "discipling leaders."

Hints & Tips

One of the biggest obstacles small group coaches encounter is group leaders who are used to going it on their own, and who don't want to be coached. It is extremely helpful to demonstrate coaching to these leaders before instituting a coaching system so they understand that the coach isn't just one more person there to tell them what to do. Building relationship between coach and coachee is also crucial.

Marriage Coaching

By Jeff Williams

Marriage Coaching is the application of Christian leadership coaching concepts and skills to facilitate growth and change for couples. The unique facet of this type of coaching is that you are working to identify and pursue growth goals that *both* partners want to attain. In this process, each individual's perspective must first be drawn out. Goals and actions are then negotiated with both partners. Sometimes, the process calls for coaching the partners individually as well as together. Another unique characteristic of marriage coaching is that sometimes the coaching itself is done by a couple, where both are coaches.

The historic paradigm for helping couples is counseling done by clinical professionals. However, coaching a couple who are able to take responsibility for their relationship, identify what they'd like to change, and develop options and actions to reach a mutual goal is much the same as coaching an individual.

Application

Helping a couple set goals differs from working with one person. Here's how to do it.

Expectations

These questions help the couple verbalize their hopes and expectations for the marriage coaching process.

- *"How did you decide to request marriage coaching? Which one of you suggested it?"*
- *"What were your first hopes about how marriage coaching might be helpful?"*
- *"How long do you expect it to take to accomplish your goals? How much time and money do you expect to invest in this process?"*
- *"What do you want to accomplish through marriage coaching that would enable you to say, 'That was a great experience, well worth all the time and effort we invested'?"*

Getting Started

The questions below are designed to help a couple settle on an agenda and set a mutually agreed-upon coaching goal.

- *"If a miracle happened tonight while you slept that solved all of your problems, what would be different tomorrow?"*
- *"What would you like to start happening or stop happening in your relationship?"*
- *"On a scale of one to ten, how would you rate your marriage in terms of overall pleasure? Explain your answer in terms of what is/isn't happening."*
- *"If there was one tool that could significantly help your relationship what would that tool do?"*
- *"What is going well that you don't want to change?"*
- *"What have you tried in the past to strengthen your relationship that has worked? That hasn't?"*
- *"What question has not been asked today that you would like to answer?"*

Marriage coaching puts a premium on paying attention to subtle intonation and body language cues, because conflicted couples sometimes refrain from explicitly disclosing their anxieties or desires out of fear of further upsetting their partners. Sometimes adding individual coaching for each partner may be necessary to facilitate open sharing.

Authors

Jeff Williams (www.GraceandTruth Relationship.com) is a marriage coach and author with years of experience working with marriages at the individual, community and national level. His wife, Jill, often coaches with him.

Transformational Coaching

By Tony Stoltzfus

Transformational Coaching is changing who you are to change what you do. It deals with a person's inner being—values, core beliefs, identity, destiny—and helps bring about deep, lasting, significant change. Clients often enter this process when they are in major life transitions (read: pain) and have become aware of their need to reinvent themselves. This type of coaching puts high demands on the coach's intuition, and draws heavily on life-stage, personality type, life purpose and other developmental tools.

Coaches who work in this area must deeply engage in their own ongoing transformational journey. It's tough to transform others when you aren't comfortable in the transformational process yourself.

Levels of Engaging

Transformational coaching often involves moving the leader through four stages of engaging (see below), representing an increasing willingness by the leader to look inward for the source of difficulty and make major identity changes. Transformation happens in the final two stages. Leaders who get stuck in the initial stages tend to "go around the mountain" and experience repeated pain until transformational change finally occurs.

1. **Endurance/Toleration**
   We focus on surviving adverse circumstances but not really learning from them.

2. **Tactical/Outward Change**
   (or engaging with the head) We make practical, external changes without taking a hard look at who we are.

3. **Engaging the Heart**
   We allow circumstances to trigger a fundamental reevaluation at the level of identity and beliefs.

4. **Overflow**
   Our transformational experience becomes a springboard for influencing many others.

Tuning Into Purpose

Often a first step in transformational coaching is helping the person move from a resistant or victim posture to one of seeing purpose in the situation. Leaders who see purpose will then embrace change instead of avoiding it.

- *"Why did this challenge come to you at this time? What is the purpose in it?"*
- *"What is God's best outcome for this situation?"*
- Challenge: *"You are only seeing this from the micro level of how it affects your own status quo. God has a much larger plan for you than that. What's a sovereign, everything-is-under-His-control, God-sized perspective on this situation?"*

- *"Let's say that God custom-designed this situation for your growth, and it is exactly what you need to move forward toward your destiny. Given that, what would you say is the purpose in this situation?"*
- *"If you walked through this and really handled it superbly, what difference would that make in your future? What would you gain?"*

Moving Beyond the Tactical (Outward Change) Level

When we *do* begin looking at ourselves, our first instinct is to engage at the doing level. For example, we examine the mistakes we made in what we did or said, or what skills we could acquire that would help us do better next time. While learning at this level is positive, it only touches on the outworkings or symptoms of what is going on inside of us. Changing what you do does not have the same transformational effect as changing who you are. The questions below can take the conversation deeper:

- *"You've identified some changes to your actions that could make a difference here. What could you change about your identity or core beliefs to transform the way you respond to situations like this?"*
- *"What do you believe about this situation? About yourself in it?"*
- *"What do your responses to your circumstances say about who you are?"*
- *"You've given me some good examples of what you've learned here on a practical level. Now let's go deeper: how does this challenge your character and core beliefs?"*
- *"Instead of engaging this at the practical level of what skills or principles you can learn, let's press in further: how does God want to reshape your identity in this?"*
- *"It feels like you are attempting to manage the consequences of the situation instead of getting at the roots. What's the root issue that gets you into situations like this in the first place?"*

Engaging with the Heart

At this level, we use the circumstances as an opportunity to for self-reflection and inner growth. Difficult experiences lay bare the heart in a way that allows transformational change—if we have the courage to really look inward and see what is there. The coaching task here is to help the person see who they are in the situation and engage that insight from the heart.

- *"How do these circumstances touch you at the place of your deepest fears, deepest desires or strongest passions?"*
- *"How can you engage this situation in terms of God's purpose for your growth in character?"*
- *"How can this situation prepare you for the great future God has called you to?"*
- *"What is driving your responses here? What is going on inside you?"*
- *"Just for the sake of argument, let's say this is 95 percent the other person's issue. What if you said, 'God, I want you to deal with me on my five percent. Give me everything you have for me in this situation!' What would that mean?"*
- *"How is Christ being incarnated in you through this?"*
- *"What is God asking of you? What part of your heart does He want to capture?"*

Quotes...

"Above all else, guard your heart; for from it flow the springs of life."

Proverbs

Authors

Tony Stoltzfus (CoachingPastors.com) specializes in helping leaders find purpose in difficult situations and be transformed by them in order to help those leaders fulfill their destiny.

Application

A look at some of the unique challenges and asking techniques of working across cultures.

Hints & Tips

In cross-cultural coaching, it's important to be proactive to avoid misunderstandings. Since many non-Western cultures handle conflict indirectly, you may not know there is a problem unless you inquire persistently, gently and without putting the client on the spot. Ask positively-framed, open questions like,

- *"What has been valuable to you in this session?"*
- *"How can I serve you more effectively?"*
- *"What do you need more/less of in our coaching relationship?"*

Cross-Cultural Coaching

By Tina Stoltzfus Horst and Paul Hillhouse

While challenging, cross-cultural coaching has great potential to enrich both the coach and client. Coaching is an excellent fit for cross-cultural interaction because, unlike counseling, mentoring or training, coaching sees the client as the expert. Cross-cultural interactions often go awry due to basic misunderstandings and differences. But because coaches help clients develop their own answers, the solutions developed in cross-cultural coaching end up naturally fitting the client's own cultural values, norms and customs.

Challenges

Coaching cross-culturally requires a high degree of self-awareness. Coaches must recognize their own cultural assumptions, and regularly check the meaning they attribute to the client. Western coaches in particular must realize that the coaching paradigm itself (which originated in the West) can have a Western bias toward individual responsibility for change and toward self-actualization. In contrast, many cultures value loyalty to and sacrifice on behalf of the community. Coaches who have cross-cultural experience tend to have an easier time understanding and accepting differing cultural paradigms.

In addition to self-awareness, coaches must also be vigilant in maintaining a learning posture as they coach cross-culturally. Humility and flexibility are tremendous assets for the coach as s/he learns from the client about the client's cultural paradigm. Learning to embrace the client's understanding of time, responsibility, identity, and how to handle conflict (to mention only a few) is essential to effectiveness. Coaches must be intentional about sticking to the coaching paradigm of asking questions rather than drawing conclusions, directing or giving advice.

Excellent cross-cultural coaches are attentive to the signs of cultural misunderstanding. Signals to be aware of are withdrawal, over-reaction/strong emotion, resistance, or confusion on either the client or coach's part. When confronted with a cultural obstacle, a posture of curiosity and the use of open questions to draw out the issue and bring understanding of it helps keep things on track.

The Sending Organization

Another important factor in cross-cultural coaching is the client's sending organization. The sending organization itself has its own corporate values, norms and customs, which may differ from both the client's own culture and the culture they are now working in. For instance, an American coach may be working with a Korean client who is an executive for a German company working in China! The coach must maintain awareness of how each layer of the cultural mix influences the coaching objectives.

Benefits

Just as the coach may be unaware of his/her cultural biases, the client's cultural paradigm may be unconscious or unexamined. Cross-cultural coaching can help clients become more aware of their own cultural paradigm, equipping them to identify cultural obstacles and to develop creative options that may never have surfaced without interacting with a coach from another culture. At times, leaders need to be transformers of culture in order to take their organization to the next level. Great cross-cultural coaches ask questions that help clients re-examine their own cultural paradigm, and this can open up new worlds for the client.

Coaching Across Cultures

- *"How would a situation like this normally be handled in your setting?"*
- *"What would a wise or mature person in this culture do in your situation?"*
- *"How do the values of your organization apply to this situation? Your personal values? The cultural values in your setting?"*
- *"What does this event or experience mean to you?"*
- *"If you choose a counter-cultural solution, what resources, support or allies might you have?"*
- *"Who besides you needs to be involved in this decision/plan/action step in order for the desired outcome to be achieved?"*

Working Across Cultures

- *"What are the cultural pressures that make it difficult for you to take the action you are considering?"*
- *"What do you stand to lose if you go against the accepted way of doing things? What might you gain?"*
- *"How far can you compromise or adapt in this situation without violating your own ethical standards and values?"*
- *"What must you do in this situation to gain trust and credibility?"*
- *"In working with people from other national or organizational cultures, where do you most typically experience frustration, confusion or conflict?"*
- *"What steps might you take in order to discover the cultural issues impacting this decision?"*

A Note on Storytelling

Storytelling is highly valued in many non-Western cultures. However, when using stories from your personal experience, be aware that the conclusion or principle you might draw from your story may not resonate with the client. When using a story, end by asking, "What did this story mean to you?" or, "What experiences have you had that helped you learn this lesson?"

Authors

Tina Stoltzfus Horst, MS, is a coach, coach trainer and therapist. She is Director of Coaching Mission International, a cross-cultural coaching non-profit. Tina@ CoachingMission. com.

Paul Hillhouse (DiscoveryL3.com) is a professional coach and recruiter who has spent the majority of his adult life living and working throughout Asia.

Topical Index

Additional Resources from Coach22.com

Below are a few examples of additional coaching and asking resources from Tony Stoltzfus, available through Coach22.com or your coaching retailer.

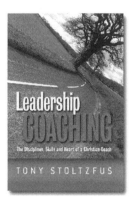

Leadership Coaching

As a complete overview of the fundamental skills and practices of coaching, *Leadership Coaching* is a great companion to this volume. Written around the Coaching Funnel conversational model (pg. 30), this book offers underlying principles and an in-depth treatment of some of the key tools found in *Coaching Questions*. Also included is an introduction to the coaching model, a look at the value system and change theory underlying the coaching approach, and a series of "Master Class" chapters that walk you through the basics of listening, asking, building support systems and more. Widely used as a basic coaching text, this book is a great place to start your coaching journey.

The Master Coach Series

These three CDs each include an hour of input and live coaching demos on a significant coaching area. They're a great choice if you want to hear some of the techniques in *Coaching Questions* in action. The first disc, *Problem Solving,* covers a variety of approaches used to generate options and come up with creative solutions without telling the client what to do. *Changing Perspective* focuses on a variety of reframing techniques that break the client out of a limited viewpoint and help them look at life situations in new ways. *Coaching Visionaries* focuses on techniques used to clarify, refine and test a visionary idea or calling.

Coaching Transitions

Life goes in cycles—from seasons where the focus is outward productivity to times of inward retooling. In this two-disc set, Tony discusses how our lack of understanding of transition causes us to try to escape these seemingly dry seasons instead of being transformed by them. We also discuss the place of suffering in fulfilling one's purpose, and how God organizes the seasons of our lives to build us into the people we were made to be. Interwoven in the input is a full length coaching session and two interviews with former coaching clients who discuss their own transitional experiences and how they found and embraced purpose within their transitions.

Made in the USA
San Bernardino, CA
24 January 2013